BUFFALO PHILHARMONIC ORCHESTRA
THE BPO CELEBRATES THE FIRST 75 YEARS

By Raya Lee & Edward Yadzinski

This book commemorating the BPO's 75th Anniversary is made possible by
Peter and Elizabeth C. Tower
Tower Family Fund, Inc.

Lead Authors: Edward Yadzinski and Raya Lee

Contributions from: Ron Daniels, Mary Kunz Goldman, Julius Kovach and Denise Prince

Contributing Editors: Richard A. Doran, Marti Gorman and Robert Pape

ISBN: 978-0-9825745-4-6

BUFFALO
HERITAGE
UNLIMITED

BuffaloHeritage.com

Published by Buffalo Heritage Unlimited, Buffalo, New York

Designed by JCharlier Communication Design   JCharlier.com

Printed by Dual Printing, Inc. in Buffalo, New York, USA   DualPrinting.com

CONTENTS

For more than a century, the cultural life of Greater Buffalo and Western New York
has prevailed over the national panorama of economic challenge and change.
Our own Buffalo Philharmonic Orchestra is exemplary, as the institution celebrates its
75th anniversary, beginning with the downbeat of the 2010-11 season.
As the curtain opens with deserved fanfare, the celebration is
first and foremost about music – the heart, soul and spirit of the BPO.

How it has all played out is a fascinating story of ideals and dreams, determination
and dedication, hard work and perseverance – all for the love of music.

**DEDICATED TO
MUSIC LOVERS OF GREATER BUFFALO**

FOREWORD

On November 7, 1935, Hungarian conductor Lajos Shuk ascended the podium in the Elmwood Music Hall, surveyed the assembled Buffalo musicians on the stage and marked the downbeat of Beethoven's *Egmont* Overture, beginning the first official concert of the Buffalo Philharmonic Orchestra.

On October 2, 2010, Music Director JoAnn Falletta took the podium in Kleinhans Music Hall, surveyed the international group of musicians who have become fellow Buffalonians over the course of the past 75 years, continuing the grand tradition which the Buffalo Philharmonic has established, and again marked the downbeat of Beethoven's *Egmont* Overture to open the Orchestra's 75th Anniversary Celebration.

This book celebrates the 75 years that the BPO has entertained Western New York audiences with a dazzling array of music including programs from the Classical Romantic and modern repertoires; "Pops" performances with such luminaries as Duke Ellington, Benny Goodman, Danny Kaye, Doc Severinsen and Marvin Hamlisch as well as Western New York's favorite Holiday Tradition – Holiday Pops; and has even collaborated with rock musicians like The Grateful Dead and Buffalo's own Ani DiFranco.

This book also honors the 75 years that the BPO has been Buffalo's cultural ambassador. Tours have brought this special part of Buffalo to Europe, Carnegie Hall, Kennedy Center, Lincoln Center and nearly every state in the Union. Radio performances are heard across the country on programs such as "Performance Today," "From The Top" and WNED's "Philharmonic Friday" and throughout Europe through distribution on the European Broadcasting Union. The BPO's recordings – recognized by two Grammy Awards in 2008 – take Buffalo to every corner of the globe through international and online distribution by NAXOS.

This book does not attempt to document the entire 75 year history of the BPO. Rather, it tells some of the many stories that illustrate why we take such immense pride in our Orchestra.

Through the continued support and dedication of the people and businesses of Western New York, the BPO begins another 75 years of beautiful music in Buffalo.

BPO*75*

BUFFALO PHILHARMONIC ORCHESTRA

A celebration of music in Buffalo, 1935-2010

PRELUDE

James D. Sheppard, owner of Sheppard's Music Store, on the site of the current Buffalo & Erie County Public Library building.

Theodore Thomas, conductor of the Theodore Thomas Orchestra

The New Music Hall was built when the German Men's Singing Societies across America chose Buffalo as their destination in 1883. Three thousand voices were heard in the new venue, accompanied by Leopold Damrosch and the New York Symphony Orchestra.

Marian de Forest
Between 1906-1935, local impresarios hosted several concert series bringing major symphony orchestras and soloists to Buffalo – Mai Davis Smith, Louis Whiting Gay, Marian de Forest, Louise Michael and Geneviev Kraft, Bessie Bellanca and Zorah Berry.

Known as the Swedish Nightingale, Jenny Lind was the most famous artist to perform during Buffalo's burgeoning years and was considered the greatest operatic soprano of the era. She performed in the old North Presbyterian Church in 1851.

Booming cannons announced the official opening of the completed Grand Erie Canal on October 26, 1825, as lavish celebrations with fireworks at every canal town in New York State continued for ten days and nights. Brisk business and easy travel brought a steady influx of European immigrants traveling west. Many would settle in Western New York, and with them came an abundance of diverse musical traditions, from folk to classical.

Canal traffic also led to various commercial ventures, one of which was Sheppard's Music Store, established in 1827 on Main Street near Eagle by James D. Sheppard. The first piano was his own, brought with him from England. The beautiful square piano enticed many new customers, and thus encouraged the beginning of musical culture in Buffalo.

Although the Native Americans who came into the store did not participate in the general music lessons or choir practice available to the public, they did come often to "hear the big music box sing."

Within seven years, Buffalo was incorporated as a city of about 10,000 residents and by 1839, the vibrant local scene enthusiastically supported a variety of first-rate local and touring entertainers. By 1850, the population of the city had quadrupled.

In November 1869, the walls of the St. James Hall echoed with two concerts by the 80-piece Theodore Thomas Orchestra, one of the greatest touring orchestras of the 19th century. Part of Thomas' mission was to introduce new American listeners to old European masters, hoping to develop and inspire audiences to form and support a professional orchestra of their own. Indeed, within a few weeks,

The Academy of Music opened on October 15, 1852 at Main and Seneca streets.

Shea's Theater on Main Street in downtown Buffalo.

Buffalo Symphony Orchestra, 1887, John Lund, Music Director

Luigi Sannella was the founding conductor of the Beethoven Symphony Orchestra in the mid 1920s. This was one of several precursors to the Buffalo Philharmonic Orchestra. Sannella led the orchestra for about six years, until the depression forced the ensemble to fold.

Beloved violinist Fritz Kreisler performed on several occasions at the Elmwood Music Hall.

Gustav Mahler performed with the New York Philharmonic in Convention Hall in Buffalo on December 7, 1910.

the first performance by a Buffalo orchestra was presented in St. James Hall, conducted by William Grosscurth.

Buffalo had become a destination for European immigrants, especially from Germany, Italy and Poland. Many of them brought their instruments from the old country and were eager to play in an ensemble. There are no detailed accounts of those rehearsals and performances, but we know that a formal balance of instruments was difficult to achieve. What was easier to assemble were choirs. The new immigrants came with their passion for singing ready to go. The most significant vocal ensembles were the German men's choirs: Buffalo Orpheus and the Schwaebischer Saengerbund. The Polish community was represented by the Moniuszko Singing Society. The Buffalo Schwaben Chor and the Polish Singing Society still sing today, carrying on these rich traditions for more than a century.

A very important part of the long, rich prelude to the founding of today's Buffalo Philharmonic Orchestra was the formation of the Buffalo Orchestra Association in 1887. Headed by Frederick C.M. Lautz, owner of the Lautz Soap

"HERR LUND PROVES TRUE ALL THAT HAS BEEN SAID OF HIM. IT WAS A DELICIOUS SENSATION TO HEAR THE PROMPT ATTACK BY A BUFFALO ORCHESTRA. EVERY SUBSCRIBER IS SATISFIED THAT HIS $12.00 IS WELL INVESTED. THERE IS SOMETHING TOUCHING IN THE AIR – IT IS THE PEOPLE."

From *The Buffalo Evening News* article "Its People Gave Buffalo a Warm Musical Heritage" about the Buffalo Symphony with conductor John Lund

Company, the Association selected John Lund for the post of music director for Buffalo's new orchestra. German-born and Leipzig-trained, Lund previously held the position of assistant conductor to the renowned Walter Damrosch at the Metropolitan Opera in New York. Known as the Buffalo Symphony Orchestra, the ensemble of 53 players performed until 1898, when the benevolent Lautz was no longer able to make up the Orchestra's deficit from the shortfalls from ticket sales and advertising.

While its future would be limited, the Buffalo Symphony Orchestra paved the way for celebrated orchestras to visit Buffalo as a major tour venue well into the 20th century.

In the winter of 1922, Buffalo's Chromatic Club sponsored the first concerts of a newly formed Buffalo Symphony Orchestra. The 70-piece ensemble was conceived by Arnold Cornelissen, who took on the role of maestro. The players were all local musicians who also played in the

MAY FESTIVAL 1912

Philharmonic Society of Buffalo

1912 May Festival Program Book May Festivals started in 1883 continued through 1917, featuring both choral and orchestral performances and offering formal concerts with handsomely produced program books. The new Music Hall at Main and Edward streets contributed greatly to the enormous success of these Festivals in Buffalo.

SIXTH CONCERT
IN SUBSCRIPTION SERIES
ELMWOOD MUSIC HALL.
Thursday Evening, March 18th, 1920.

Philadelphia
Symphony Orchestra
LEOPOLD STOKOWSKI,
Conductor

Programme

The
DETROIT
SYMPHONY
ORCHESTRA

OSSIP GABRILOWITSCH
Conductor
presented by
BUFFALO MUSICAL
FOUNDATION
INCORPORATED
Monday Evening
December 3rd, 1934
at
Elmwood Music Hall

Elmwood Music Hall, later known as Convention Hall
was located at Elmwood Avenue and Virginia Street.

John Philip Sousa
The John Philip Sousa Band's
many performances in the Temple
of Music during June and
July 1901 included the premiere
of his *Invincible Eagle March*,
composed for the City of Buffalo.

The Temple of Music, the
center of all major events
during the Pan-American
Exposition in 1901.

Buffalo Symphony Orchestra program, with
John Ingram conducting, broadcast over WBEN radio.

very popular movie houses and vaudeville theaters
throughout Western New York.

The Buffalo Symphony Orchestra under Cornelissen
might have eventually become a fully professional
orchestra had it not been limited by its "local musicians
only" policy. The concept was well-intended and initially
supported by concert presenters including Mai Davis
Smith and her successor, Marian de Forest, who
circulated what was known as The Buffalo Plan in 1924.
This remarkable document states, "Not only is it the
intent to fill every place in the orchestra with local
musicians, but also to employ only soloists living in
Buffalo for the concerts. Our first step must be a complete abandonment
of the idea of a full-time orchestra, concurred by the public, the financial
backers, the musicians, conductor and manager." After various starts and stops,
the idea ultimately proved to be impractical, although Mai Davis Smith and
Marian de Forest must be credited with setting the stage for a permanent
orchestra with an emphasis on concerts for both adults and children.

The name "Buffalo Symphony Orchestra" emerged
again in 1932. This time the roots took hold, as
75 players volunteered to form a professional-level
orchestra, with a new maestro on the podium. John
Ingram, who had emigrated from Holland just five years
earlier, conducted the first concert in the Elmwood Music
Hall on April 30, 1932. Ingram had been conducting
theater orchestras in Buffalo, including Shea's. Musicians
were happy for the theater work, but felt their technique
for classical repertoire was wanting. Under Ingram, the
same ensemble performed under a variety of names,
including the Buffalo Civic Orchestra, the Buffalo
Community Orchestra, and finally, the Buffalo
Philharmonic Orchestra. It was under the latter name that the ensemble was
designated as the official orchestra for Buffalo's 1932 centennial celebration.

Finally, after more than 60 years of well-intended efforts, the current Buffalo
Philharmonic Orchestra was formally founded in the fall of 1935. From that
moment 75 years ago, the people of Greater Buffalo have loved and supported
their symphony orchestra with pride.

CHAPTER 1
THE SHUK YEARS
1935-1937

LAJOS SHUK

BORN
April 5, 1897
Budapest, Hungary

STUDIED
Cello, piano, composition,
conducting

DIED
June 24, 1962
Los Angeles, California

FIRST BPO CONCERT
November 7, 1935
Beethoven - *Egmont Overture, op.8*
Brahms - *Symphony No.3 in F major, op.90*
Debussy - *Two Nocturnes*
Gliere - *Russian Sailor's Dance*

LAST CONCERT AS MUSIC DIRECTOR
March 11, 1937
Mozart - *La Clemenza di Tito: Overture*
Reger - *Variations and Fugue
on a Theme by Mozart*
Mahler - *Adagietto from Symphony No.5*
Enesco - *Roumanian Rhapsody No.1 in
A major, op.11*
Beethoven - *Piano Concerto No.5
in E-flat major, op. 73 "Emperor"*
    Harold Bauer, pianist
Strauss J.Jr. - *Emperor Waltzes*

UNIVERSITY OF CALIFORNIA, BERKELEY, BANCROFT LIBRARY COLLECTION

BUFFALO HIGHLIGHTS
- Conducted the first BPO Youth Concert
  on December 17, 1935

CAREER HIGHLIGHTS
- Cello virtuoso – performed on European
  and American tours; recorded in Los
  Angeles for film scores and studio work
- Radio broadcasts on WABC from Buffalo
- Led the Boston Pops on a 1957
  Florida Tour
- Studied composition with Zoltan Kodaly,
  and later took private lessons in
  conducting with Felix Weingartner
  and Bruno Walter

"Music has a wonderful power of bringing persons together. If it has an international spread, music can do much toward cementing
firmer relationships between various races of people. The International League of Composers attempts to do this very thing."

- LAJOS SHUK, *BUFFALO TIMES*, MARCH 15, 1936

THE SHUK YEARS

1935-1937

BPO MUSICIANS 1935-36

VIOLIN I
Jan Wolanek, Concertmaster
Erich Beu
Martin Thomsen
Arthur Snelgrove
Albert Greenberg
John Metschl
Erich Hechter
Albert Koch
John Geerts
George Elflein
Arthur Fleury
George Critchley

VIOLIN II
Alexander Fischer
Morris Cheskin
George Kolger
Emanuel Greenberg
Alfred Raeppel
Irving Tallis
Arthur Schwarzott
Oscar Witte

Frank Gans
Richard Krege
Arthur Haendeges
Stanley Mikulec

VIOLA
Fred Ressel
Adam Federlein
Ivan Shapiro
Edward Dittrich
Eugene Kappler
Fred Krafft
William Zacharias
Cornelius Boulange

CELLO
Frank McGoldrick
Wilhelm Schmidt
Nicholas D'Addio
Arnold Cornelissen
Sam Masling
Leonard D'Anna
Raymond Frey
Fred Caster

STRING BASS
Henry Sticht
Philip Millonzi
Frederick Brabez
Paul Hennig
Nelson Muszynski
Edward Radel
Homer Cline

FLUTE
Edward Hall
Jose Acosta
Leopold Roebbig

PICCOLO
Leopold Roebbig

OBOE
Carl Bernhardt
Anthony Grimaldi

ENGLISH HORN
Anthony Grimaldi

CLARINET
Theodore Bouczek
William Robinson
John Buchar

CONTRABASSOON
William Wisler
Herbert Reich

FRENCH HORN
Joseph Hayne
Herbert Flumerfeldt
Frederick Holcomb
Charles Jepson

TRUMPET
Louis Impellieter
Harry Wooler
August Luebcke
Ernest Barton

TROMBONE
Angelo Tulumello
Raymond Ditch
Albert Demske

TUBA
William Montheith

HARP
Laura Lambrix

TIMPANI
Milton Kiener

PERCUSSION
Louis Losson
Edmund Oroschin
Edward Adams
Harold Tapson

NOTABLE GUEST CONDUCTORS

Arnold Cornelissen, composer and guest conductor | January 23, 1936

Creighton Churchill, conductor | May 3, 1936

Frank Foti, conductor | May 10, 1936

NOTABLE SOLOISTS

C. Gordon Watkins, pianist | November 18, 1935

Harold Bradley, pianist | January 9, 1936

Russell Baum, composer, pianist | February 6, 1936

Raymond Cook, baritone | February 20, 1936

Jeanne Gautier, violinist | March 5, 1936

Audrey Ely, soprano | March 29, 1936

Florence Ann Reid, contralto | March 29, 1936

Guy Maier, pianist | April 19, 1936

Mischa Elman, violinist | November 5, 1936

Anna Kaskas, contralto | December 2, 1936

Amy Corey Pomeroy, pianist | January 7, 1937

Harold Bauer, pianist | March 11, 1937

CHAIRMAN OF THE BPO BOARD OF DIRECTORS

1936-1939 Mrs. Edgar F. Wendt

THE SHUK YEARS

1935-1937

Soup lines. Bank failures. Unprecedented unemployment. It was the height of the Great Depression in Buffalo and throughout the nation. Despite the frigid economic climate in the 1930s, Buffalo was nevertheless warming up to the idea of having its own professional symphony orchestra. Fortunately, the city had some laurels to rest on. Among the largest and wealthiest cities in the nation, Buffalo boasted community leaders with the savvy and wherewithal to make it happen. Some of the city's most celebrated names, including Cameron Baird, Samuel Capen and Frederick Slee, recognized that a federal program known as the "ERB" might be just the ticket to underwrite some of the costs of transitioning the ad-hoc symphonic concerts taking place in Buffalo into a professional, fully-contracted season.

In 1934, a brilliant young conductor and cellist from Budapest was recruited to Buffalo to help community planners establish a major symphony orchestra in Western New York. The new orchestra opened its first official season in the fall of 1935. The BPO planners sought support from the Federal Emergency Relief Bureau, which sponsored the appointment of Lajos Shuk to oversee the many artistic and administrative decisions vital to a major symphonic institution. With extensive European training, Shuk had already served as the conductor of the New York Civic Orchestra.

Shuk was appointed director of Buffalo's Emergency Relief Bureau (ERB) Orchestra, one of several cultural public works programs sponsored by the United States government.

BPO Conductor Lajos Shuk (*left*) and Associate Conductor Theophil Wendt (no relation to Mrs. Edgar F. Wendt).

He moved quickly to settle on the Buffalo Philharmonic Orchestra as a permanent name, under which he assembled the finest players in Western New York. As a prelude to the future orchestra, various classics, children's, family and Pops programs were offered through the spring of 1935, with 24 broadcasts on WABC national radio network, beginning with a program on March 2, 1935.

By August 1935, federal Works Progress Administration (WPA) funding was also secured for Buffalo's new orchestra, with support from WPA administrator Nikolai Sokoloff, the former maestro of the Cleveland Symphony Orchestra. Anticipating that funding, the orchestra planned its first season while simultaneously launching an aggressive funding campaign to pay remaining expenses. To tie the ribbons on

continued on page 8

WPA AND THE BPO

The United States and most of the world were mired in the depths of the Great Depression, but the inauguration of Franklin D. Roosevelt brought immense change to the United States. Among FDR's many social and economic programs were two which ultimately had a profound effect on the future of Buffalo and the Buffalo Philharmonic Orchestra: the ERB and the WPA.

Established in 1934, the Emergency Relief Bureau (ERB) was specifically designed to support theater projects, and theaters needed music. Funding was paid directly to cities. The Buffalo Emergency Relief Bureau Orchestra under Lajos Shuk was funded through the Theater Workshop Department. As a curious spinoff, there was also a Puppet & Marionette Theater, one of several departments required to depict a story about our local history.

FDR established the Works Projects Administration (WPA) in 1935 to create jobs at a time when unemployment had reached unprecedented levels. The WPA's broad programs provided funds to help construct thousands of new buildings, bridges, roadways and up-grades to airports.

In Buffalo, War Memorial Auditorium, the Zoo and Kleinhans all relied heavily on WPA funds and support. In addition to infrastructure, however, the WPA also provided support for the Federal Art, Writers and Theatre Projects. Innovative music programs paid a portion of

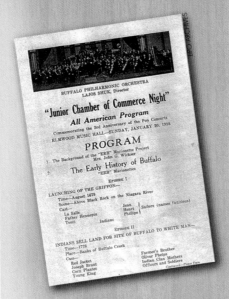

ERB Puppet Theater presented "A History of Early Buffalo"

Cameron Baird, businessman and community leader who helped found the BPO and the UB Music Department.

Mrs. Edgar F. Wendt, BPO Society President, oversaw the first BPO Campaign Fund Drive in 1935, allowing the orchestra to continue the 1935-36 season until WPA funding was in place.

Zorah B. Berry, Buffalo Philharmonic Orchestra Concert Manager

Soloists scheduled during the 1938-39 season, Franco Autori conductor. (*From left*) pianist Rudolf Serkin, violinist Efrem Zimbalist, baritone David B. McCloskey, cellist Emanuel Feuermann and soprano Marjorie Lawrence. *The Buffalo Evening News* identified the BPO as "the Buffalo Orchestra of the WPA federal music project under the sponsorship of the Buffalo Philharmonic Orchestra Society" in this 1938 article, well after the official BPO incorporation in 1936.

Construction is underway on Buffalo's new music hall. Note the PWA sign in the foreground indicating federal relief funding.

PWA
FEDERAL WORKS AGENCY
PUBLIC WORKS ADMINISTRATION
KLEINHANS MUSIC HALL

M. SHAPIRO & SON
CONSTRUCTION COMPANY, INC.
ENGINEERS AND CONTRACTORS
753 7TH AVE. NEW YORK CITY
ELECTRICAL
WORK
PLUMBING
HEATING
GEO. H. DRAKE

WPA
FEDERAL MUSIC PROJECT
DR. NIKOLAI SOKOLOFF
Federal Director

BUFFALO
PHILHARMONIC
ORCHESTRA

LAJOS SHUK
Conducting

Season 1935-1936
YOUNG PEOPLES CONCERT

THE FEDERAL MUSIC PROJECT
of the
WORKS PROGRESS ADMINISTRATION
presents
THE BUFFALO ORCHESTRA
FRANCO AUTORI
CONDUCTING
PAUL HINDEMITH
ASSISTING ARTIST

STATE TEACHERS COLLEGE
FRIDAY EVENING, APRIL 23, 1937
AT 8:45 O'CLOCK

W. S. BRISTER
DISTRICT SUPERVISOR
106 CITY HALL, BUFFALO, N.Y.

The Program
YOUNG PEOPLES CONCERT
DECEMBER TWENTY-FIRST

Soloists: Walter Hagen, Violin, and the Buffalo Children's Chorus
under direction of William Breach

I.   WASHINGTON POST MARCH . . . . Sousa
II. LARGO "FROM THE NEW WORLD" SYMPHONY . . Dvorak
III. The string instrument explained and demonstrated
     LAJOS SHUK
IV. a. TRAUMEREI for strings only . . . . . Schumann
     b. CAPRICE VIENNOIS . . . . Kreisler
     c. MOLLY ON THE SHORE, Irish Reel . . Grainger

INTERMISSION

V.   RONDO CAPRICCIOSO for Violin and Orchestra . . Saint-Saens
     Soloist: WALTER HAGEN
VI. CHRISTMAS CAROLS . . . . English Carol
     a. WASSAIL! WASSAIL! . . . . Martin Shaw
     b. OLD CHRISTMAS . . . . Traditional
     c. OH, COME ALL YE FAITHFUL
     BUFFALO CHILDREN'S CHORUS, WILLIAM BREACH, Director
VII. TALES FROM THE VIENNA WOODS, Valse . . Johann Strauss

ACKNOWLEDGMENTS
To Mr. William Breach, Director of Music, Board of
Education for his co-operation

KLEINH
F.J. & W.A.
M. SHAPIRO
GENERAL

Gives Verdict

Nikolai Sokoloff,
former conductor
of the Cleveland
Symphony
Orchestra and
national director
of music projects
for the Federal
Works Progress
Administration
(WPA).

COURIER EXPRESS, AUGUST 8, 1935

From the *Courier Express*, August 8, 1935

ERB Musicians Win Reward of Lengthy Struggle in Noted Conductor's Praise

The Buffalo Philharmonic Orchestra gave a private recital in Elmwood Music Hall yesterday for one of America's most famous symphony conductors... His appearance transformed the routine morning rehearsal into an event of outstanding importance. After they performed, Dr. Nikolai Sokoloff approached the podium. All were silent: "I have never heard anything half so fine among the orchestras that are playing as you are, under adverse conditions," he said. "I had no idea you could play so well. This is not empty flattery. I conducted the Cleveland Symphony for 15 years and I have heard or conducted every orchestra of importance in the country."

What Dr. Sokoloff's quiet tribute meant to 100 men who have struggled along on relief wages for a year or more was made clear when he concluded a few minutes later. The Buffalo Philharmonic Orchestra would receive high recommendation to receive WPA funding and support for a permanent orchestra.

The 100 men rose in an ovation in which they themselves felt a share, and frank tears of gratified happiness were visible on many faces.

musicians' salaries, as in the case of the Buffalo Philharmonic Orchestra.

Under the auspices of WPA, 104 Buffalo musicians were assigned to six music units, one of which was the newly established Buffalo Philharmonic Orchestra. Programs ranged from popular dance music to classical recitals and were presented weekly to hospitals, schools, community houses and centers throughout the city. There were also concerts given twice a month in Elmwood Music Hall and the Statler Ballroom, and weekly afternoon concerts at the Albright Art Gallery.

Just before her passing in 1935, Marian de Forest remarked to BPO benefactor Florence Wendt about the impending support from the WPA: "It seems, according to all the letters pouring in to me from the musical authorities of this country regarding the musicianship and accomplishments of Lajos Shuk, that now is our golden opportunity and that the man is here who can accomplish this job of building up a permanent orchestra for Buffalo. It is my great desire to work to this end."

WPA support encouraged the Greater Buffalo community to rally behind the new BPO and plan for a future of great music-making.

Maestro Shuk fit right into
Buffalo's multicultural society.
He spoke candidly with Buffalo
newspapers about leaving his home
in Budapest for Berlin to solo with
the Berlin Philharmonic. It was
during the revolution, and all
public services were curtailed—
there were no lights, no heat,
no transportation. Despite his parents'
worries, he set out with his cello,
a small stove and a can of oil.
In Berlin, he played to a sold-out house.
When the audience would not
stop applauding, the stage managers
turned off the lights, to no avail.
It was not until the young cellist had
played three unaccompanied encores
that the audience allowed him to leave.
For his services, Shuk received the vital
payment of a 200-pound bag of flour.

COURIER EXPRESS, MARCH 1936

COURIER EXPRESS, MARCH 1936

Studied Music Between Bombings

Lajos Shuk Faced Revolutions, Now Directs Buffalo Philharmonic

Lajos Shuk directs—
(right) "All together."
(center) "Violins, violins!"
(left) "Smoother now."
A campaign to raise $75,000 to make the orchestra permanent begins tomorrow.

Montage of Buffalo
Philharmonic Orchestra's new
conductor on the podium.

the start-up first season, and with an eye on a long future, the Buffalo Philharmonic Orchestra Society was incorporated in the spring of 1936.

The evening of November 7, 1935 at Elmwood Music Hall was the auspicious Opening Night for the BPO's first season. Under Shuk's direction, the program derived from European tradition and began with Beethoven's *Egmont* Overture, followed by the lush resonance of Brahms' Symphony No.3 and the Impressionist colors of Debussy's *Two Nocturnes*. With a lighter touch, the concert closed with Glière's swaggering *Russian Sailor's Dance*.

Public reaction was immensely favorable, and the Orchestra was off and running to meet the ideals of its mission statement, which reads virtually the same today:

The Buffalo Philharmonic Orchestra Society, Inc. will provide a resident, professional, major symphony orchestra of artistic excellence and integrity to enrich the quality of life in Western New York through the presentation of live symphonic music and other musical events which will educate and entertain the broadest possible audiences within and beyond the Western New York region.

COURIER EXPRESS

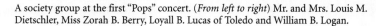

A society group at the first "Pops" concert. (*From left to right*) Mr. and Mrs. Louis M. Dietschler, Miss Zorah B. Berry, Loyall B. Lucas of Toledo and William B. Logan.

BPO ARCHIVES

ELMWOOD
MUSIC
HALL

•

THIRD SEASON

POPS

•

Buffalo Philharmonic Orchestra

•

LAJOS SHUK
DIRECTOR

ELMWOOD
MUSIC
HALL

COURIER EXPRESS, MARCH 17, 1937

Men You Ought to Know

By H. KATHERINE SMITH

"Men You Ought to Know," according to the *Courier Express* in March 1937 included Robert Thompson, Fredonia Normal School; John W. Henry, bicycle shop owner; and Lajos Shuk.

Within weeks of its opening Classics concert, the Buffalo Philharmonic began to deliver on one of its most important functions: bringing great music to young ears.

The BPO presented its very first education concert on December 17, 1935, appropriately presented by the Music Department of the Buffalo Public Schools. The program featured the *Ruy Blas* Overture and Piano Concerto in G minor, Op.25 by Mendelssohn, and an inspirational cantata, *The Golden Legend* by Sir Arthur Sullivan.

Without missing a beat, the BPO followed just four days later with its first Young People's Concert, featuring the music of Sousa, Dvořák, Schumann, Kreisler, Grainger and Johann Strauss Jr., including a performance of Saint-Saëns' *Rondo Capriccioso* with violin soloist Walter Hagen. A seasonal medley of Christmas carols was included for good measure. The value of the program – then, as it is today – is that young children and students have an opportunity to hear great masterpieces played by a live orchestra.

At the time, Shuk was considered to be a modernist, often selecting the music of Ravel, Debussy, Strauss and Stravinsky. He also made a point of performing American music and was proud to report that he played tennis with George Gershwin.

As the Buffalo Philharmonic took shape under Shuk's leadership, the community buzzed with new energy, forming committees to sponsor choral singing, chamber music, dancing and children's concerts. All of this was supported by various lectures on music appreciation.

In January 1936, the new orchestra was put to the test. The famous

Elmwood Music Hall, located on Elmwood Avenue at Virginia Street, was demolished in 1938.

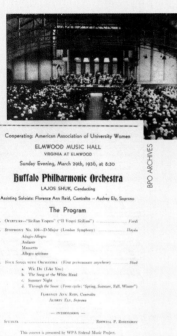

Lajos Shuk conducting the BPO in Elmwood Music Hall.

Cleveland Orchestra had unexpectedly cancelled its February 4 performance in the Elmwood Music Hall, and the fledgling BPO was forced to fill in. Support came from prominent members of the community and BPO Board members who wrote letters that appeared in the *Courier Express* encouraging music lovers to purchase tickets despite the last-minute change. The concert was nearly sold out. It was clear that Buffalo audiences were ready to accept their "local" symphony orchestra as first-rate.

Shuk's second and final season as the maestro of the Buffalo Philharmonic was a bit unusual. In part to honor his achievements during the BPO's first year, the Buffalo Philharmonic Orchestra Society engaged the renowned violinist Mischa Elman to perform Tchaikovsky's Violin Concerto

Violinist Mischa Elman was a guest soloist in November 1936.

on opening night, November 5, 1936. Later that season under Shuk, Harold Bauer performed Beethoven's *"Emperor"* Piano Concerto No. 5 on March 11, 1937.

In all, Shuk conducted just five concerts that season, allowing his eventual successor, Franco Autori, to establish his credentials with Buffalo's concert-going public. In fact, Autori had been brought to Buffalo as part of the new Federal Music Project, funded by Franklin D. Roosevelt's Works Progress Administration (WPA).

It was a critical time, but from the very first performance, the Society's Board of Directors got everything right. Shuk's musicianship and dedication to the orchestra and to the community was deeply appreciated. He moved on to continue a successful performing and conducting career on the West Coast.

CHAPTER 2

THE AUTORI YEARS

1937-1945

FRANCO AUTORI

BORN
November 29, 1903
Naples, Italy

STUDIED
Piano, violin, composition

DIED
October 16, 1990
Tulsa, Oklahoma

FIRST BPO CONCERT
November 8, 1936
Beethoven - *Leonore Overture No.3, op.72*
Brahms - *Symphony No.4 in E minor, op.98*
Debussy - *Two Nocturnes*
Wagner - *Tannhäuser: Overture*

LAST CONCERT AS MUSIC DIRECTOR
March 20, 1945
Rimsky-Korsakoff - *Russian Easter Overture*
Mozart - *Violin Concerto No.3 in G major, K.216*
   Ariana Bronstein, violinist
Copland - *Lincoln Portrait*
   Carl Sandburg, narrator
Stravinsky - *Firebird Suite*

RETURN BPO ENGAGEMENTS
April 19 & 20, 1970
November 16, 1985 – 50th Anniversary Concert

BPO ARCHIVES

BUFFALO HIGHLIGHTS
- Conducted opening concert in Kleinhans Music Hall, October 12, 1940

CAREER HIGHLIGHTS
- Emigrated to the United States in 1928
- Summer Conductor, Dallas Symphony 1932-1934
- Music Director, Chautauqua Institute 1943-1953
- Associate Conductor, New York Philharmonic, 1949-1959
- Music Director, Tulsa Symphony, 1961-1971

"When I first arrived in Buffalo I was met by many photographers, many reporters. I was tired and unshaven but had to face many questions like 'Who was my favorite composer?' The reporters pressed me for some examples, so I said, 'Well, music like Bach, Beethoven, Mozart and Wagner.' The next day I opened one of the newspapers and there were four pictures of me on the front page! I was so unshaven I looked like a murderer. And the caption under the pictures said: 'Italian-born conductor prefers German music.' All at once, more than 90,000 Italian-American residents of Buffalo were mad at me."

- FRANCO AUTORI, 1935

THE AUTORI YEARS

1937-1945

KLEINHANS OPENING NIGHT BPO PERSONNEL

VIOLIN I
Joseph Wincenc, Concertmaster
Frank Plagge
Louis Podgorski
Martin Thomsen
Wallace Michalski
Erich Beu
William Schimpf
Albert Greenberg
Meyer Balsom
June Hards
Isadore Prince
Joseph Romano
Stanley Mikulec
Max Sittenfeld

VIOLIN II
Arthur Snelgrove
Arthur Lundequist
George Kolger
Morris Cheskin
Erich Hechter
Paul Muni

Isidor Termini
Jan Geerts
Matthew Tworek
Emanuel Greenberg

VIOLA
Fred A. Ressel
Ivan Shapiro
Edward Gerstel
Edward Dittrich
Eugene Kappler
Walter Raszeja
William Zacharias

CELLO
Rudolf Doblin
William Fahlbusch
Samuel Masling
Nicholas D'Addio
Fred Caster
Frank McGoldrick
Wilhelm Schmidt

STRING BASS
Martin Danzscher
Homer Cline
Max Rauschstadt
Fred Yutzinski
Nelson Muczynski
Cross Maggio

FLUTE
Paige Brook
Ort L. Bachelor
Leopold Roebbig

PICCOLO
Leopold Roebbig

OBOE
Ezra Kotzin
Antonio Grimaldi
Carl Bernhardt

ENGLISH HORN
Antonio Grimaldi

CLARINET
Raymond Fiutak
Harvey R. Prather
Frank Rosselli

BASS CLARINET
Frank Rosselli

BASSOON
William G. Wisler
Herbert Reich

FRENCH HORN
Fred Holcomb
Herbert J. Flumerfeldt
Joseph Hayn
Charles H. Jepson

TRUMPET
Louis Impellieter
Conrad Stellar
August Luebcke

TROMBONE
Angelo Tulumello
Santolo Carriero
Albert Demske

TUBA
Nelson Muszynski

TIMPANI
August Stoerr

PERCUSSION
Edmund Oroschin
Edward Adams
Louis Losson

HARP
Laura Lambrix

PIANO, CELESTE & ORGAN
Squire Haskin

NOTABLE GUEST CONDUCTORS

Paul Hindemith, composer, violist, conductor | April 23, 1937

Percy Grainger, composer, pianist, conductor | November 30, 1943

NOTABLE GUEST SOLOISTS

Harold Bauer, pianist | April 19, 1938

Efrem Zimbalist, violinist | February 7, 1939

Rudolf Serkin, pianist | April 25, 1939

Benny Goodman, clarinetist | November 5, 1939

Albert Spaulding, violinist | March 6, 1941

Joseph Szigeti, violinist | February 17, 1942

Lotte Lehmann, soprano | December 1, 1942

Misha Mischakoff, violinist | March 2, 1943

Anne Brown, soprano | March 21, 1943

Joseph Hofmann, pianist | March 29, 1943

Paul Wittgenstein, pianist | February 29, 1944

Jennie Tourel, mezzo-soprano | November 28, 1944

Mischa Elman, violinist | January 23, 1945

CHAIRMEN OF THE BPO BOARD OF DIRECTORS

1936-1939 Mrs. Edgar F. Wendt

1940-1941 Mrs. Carlton M. Smith

1942-1943 Hon. Charles B. Sears

1944-1946 Mr. James How

THE AUTORI YEARS

1937-1945

In the early 1930s, the refrigerator may have been the most important appliance in the home, but the radio was the most glamorous. In 1937, the NBC Symphony was created for one of the greatest conductors of the era: Arturo Toscanini. There were a few surprises along the way, like the panic in 1938 caused by a radio broadcast by Orson Welles when he staged a radio version of H.G. Wells' novel, *War of the Worlds*. Although there were many musical interludes, thousands of listeners believed the story of Martians landing on earth. Radio was a powerful force indeed.

The BPO was heard on local radio stations from the mid- to late-1930s. This spoke volumes for the Orchestra's artistic future. But the future needed to be planned and funded. No one took the responsibility for meeting the Orchestra's continuing economic needs more to heart than BPO Society president Florence Wendt, known as Mrs. Edgar F. Wendt. Under her leadership, an extraordinary public campaign raised $35,000, enough to keep the Orchestra going through the 1937-38 season, until federal WPA funding promised by Dr. Nikolai Sokoloff arrived.

The WPA had already recruited Franco Autori, a conductor from the Dallas Symphony, who had been dispatched to Buffalo for the BPO's second season in 1936-37. During that concert year, while Shuk held the title of music director, Autori functioned as a resident guest conductor. He was appointed as BPO music director

BPO ARCHIVE

BUFFALO PHILHARMONIC
Orchestra **FRANCO AUTORI** *Conductor*

THIRD SYMPHONY CONCERT
TUESDAY, DECEMBER 15, 1942, 8:45 P.M.
KLEINHANS MUSIC HALL
WITH BUFFALO PHILHARMONIC CHORUS

at the beginning of the 1937-38 season. The WPA funds Autori brought with him also allowed additional players to be hired, as well as a broadly expanded series of 21 concerts in 1936-37 season.

Under Autori, the Orchestra presented many fine symphonic performances with renowned soloists, and began performing run-out concerts to Niagara Falls and Akron, New York. Elmwood Music Hall was demolished in 1938 and concerts were held in the Buffalo Consistory (now Canisius High School).

Although natural growing pains led to a variety of administrative and financial issues over the 1937-38 and 1938-39 seasons, by the opening of the 1939-40 season, even without WPA support, the BPO Society and the Greater Buffalo community was able to expand its classical, Pops and educational programming, all under Autori's confident baton. The prospect of a world-class home in the new music

POSTCARD IMAGE FROM CHUCK LACHIUSA

Buffalo Consistory at 1180 Delaware Avenue, once the private residence of George Rand and now part of Canisius High School.

The Buffalo Consistory was the old Rand Mansion on Delaware Avenue. There, in this private home, was an auditorium. On one occasion Rudolf Serkin performed, I think the C Minor Concerto of Mozart. On the ceiling of this little auditorium were stars; it had a kind of heavenly effect when the lights were dimmed...

- **ROBERT I. MILLONZI**

BPO ARCHIVES

The
**Buffalo
Philharmonic
Orchestra**

•

Franco Autori
Conductor

•

SYMPHONY SERIES
1940-41

•

in

KLEINHANS
MUSIC HALL

EVERYBODY'S DAILY NEWSPAPER (IN POLISH), B&ECPL SCRAPBOOKS

A montage of musicians, including Stanley Mikulec, Matthew Tworek and Raymond Dyczkowski that appeared in the Polish newspaper *Everybody's Daily*.

hall under construction on Richmond and Porter avenues surely helped fuel community support for the BPO during these tenuous years as the nation began to emerge from the Great Depression.

In 1940, Autori directed the gala debut concert for Kleinhans Music Hall, which opened its doors to the

EACH MEMBER OF THE ORCHESTRA RECEIVED $18 A WEEK. IMAGINE THAT! THE FIRST CHAIR PEOPLE RECEIVED $21 A WEEK, AND I (AS ASSISTANT CONCERTMASTER) HAD THE MOST FABULOUS SALARY OF $25 A WEEK!"

- **DR. JOSEPH A. WINCENC**

public on October 12. The program began with Autori's own orchestral adaptation of Bach's celebrated Toccata and Fugue in D minor. After intermission, the Orchestra continued with Beethoven's Violin Concerto in D major featuring Buffalo's own Eudice Shapiro as soloist, and concluded with Brahms' epic Symphony No.1 in C minor.

BPO ARCHIVES

1940-41 Gala debut season brochure, the BPO's first in the new Kleinhans Music Hall.

THE BUFFALO EVENING NEWS, OCTOBER 20, 1942

The war years in Buffalo mirrored those of any other city in the U.S. As the icon, Rosie the Riveter worked her way into factories and women were starting to land jobs as professional musicians. The number of women musicians in the BPO tripled in 1942, and by 1945, more than a dozen female musicians played under Franco Autori's baton.

THE BUFFALO EVENING NEWS, NOVEMBER 20, 1942

The impressive violin section for a WBEN broadcast.

Music of eight of the United Nations was featured in a one-hour program presented as a public service by *The Buffalo Evening News* and broadcast on WBEN on November 20, 1942. This was one of a series of five such concerts, and the second year in a row that the series was broadcast. Maestro and Mrs. Autori invited dozens of guests to their Franklin Street home to listen to these broadcasts and discuss the concerts. Concert attendance increased.

Another well-known violinist from Western New York on the stage that evening was Joseph Wincenc, who began his tenure as the Orchestra's assistant concert master and later was named associate conductor of the BPO.

In addition to attracting and selecting many fine musicians for the Orchestra, Autori took care

BUFFALO'S APPETITE FOR POPS PROGRAMMING STEMMED FROM THE VIBRANT JAZZ SCENE, WITH LEGENDARY MUSICIANS APPEARING REGULARLY AT THE COLORED MUSICIANS CLUB, THE ANCHOR BAR, THE STATLER BALLROOM AND MANY OTHER AREA HOTSPOTS.

to expand the BPO's classical repertoire. Among the celebrated performers who appeared with the BPO were jazz great Benny Goodman, who performed Mozart's Clarinet Concerto, as well as violinists Efrem Zimbalist and Joseph Szigeti, tenor John Priebe, mezzo-soprano Jennie Tourel and pianists Rudolf Serkin,

continued on page 20

KLEINHANS OPENS!

"The shape of the violin has derived from its function as a musical instrument. A concert auditorium, in its most intimate nature, is likewise a musical instrument."

- E. SAARINEN

A new era was at hand. The sound of music accompanied by the rumble of passing trolley cars – the mark of the old Elmwood Music Hall – was almost over. The generous donation of the $1 million estate of businessman Edward L. Kleinhans and his wife, Mary Seaton Kleinhans, with some additional Federal Emergency Relief Administration of Public Works (PWA) funds, would provide Buffalo with one of the world's finest music halls. The jobs generated by this construction project were undoubtedly also very welcome during these Depression years.

The search for a new concert hall site began in the early 1930s. Buffalo architect E.B. Green submitted a neoclassical design that would have made the hall an enormous addition to the Buffalo Museum of Science. Ultimately, the Truman Avery mansion site on The Circle at Richmond and Porter avenues was chosen.

Kleinhans' executor and chairman of the Buffalo Foundation, George F. Rand, hired architects F.J. and William Kidd, in May, 1938. Then, in stepped Esther Link, a well-traveled high school music teacher and passionate devotee of architecture, who was disappointed in the Kidd drawings shown to her by Buffalo Foundation lawyer, Edward P. Letchworth, calling them "a disaster." Letchworth asked her to write out her thoughts. Rand and fellow board member Philip Wickser paid very close attention to her reasoning and were especially impressed by pictures of buildings designed by Finnish architect Eliel Saarinen that she provided. At Letchworth's request, Link drafted an impassioned plea to

Sergei Koussevitsky (*left*), conductor of the Boston Symphony Orchestra, with Eliel Saarinen, architect of Kleinhans Music Hall.

EDWARD L. KLEINHANS   MARY SEATON KLEINHANS

THIS MUSIC HALL IS DEDICATED TO THE MEMORY OF MARY LIVINGSTON KLEINHANS, THE MOTHER, AND MARY SEATON KLEINHANS, THE WIFE OF EDWARD L. KLEINHANS IN HONOR OF THEM IT IS TO BE PERPETUALLY KNOWN AS THE KLEINHANS MUSIC HALL IT COMMEMORATES THE PUBLIC SPIRIT, THE VISION AND THE GENEROSITY OF EDWARD L. AND MARY S. KLEINHANS, WHO DEVOTED THEIR ENTIRE ESTATES TO THE BUILDING OF THIS CENTER OF MUSICAL CULTURE FOR THE USE, ENJOYMENT AND BENEFIT OF THE PEOPLE OF THE CITY OF BUFFALO

Dedicatory Plaque in Foyer of Hall

SECOND SEASON, 1940-41
FIFTH SYMPHONY PROGRAM, JANUARY NINTH   5

Invitation to Opening Night in Kleinhans Music Hall.

View of the Kleinhans stage from the balcony.

In 1924, Buffalo's Chopin Singing Society commissioned the bronze statue of Frederic Chopin from sculptor Joseph C. Mazur. Mounted on a granite base, the work stands today on the outer grounds of Kleinhans Music Hall at Symphony Circle facing east.

A snowy, winter view of the Kleinhans grounds.

A contemporary view of Kleinhans Music Hall.

A stark, late afternoon look at Kleinhans in the fall.

VERDI

A lovely watercolor of Kleinhans Music Hall by the BPO's own JoAnn Falletta.

Also on the Kleinhans grounds, facing north, is a bronze statue of Guiseppe Verdi, by sculptors Antonio Ugo and A. Decianno, erected in 1907 by the Italian-American community of Buffalo.

Saarinen in July, 1938, and the Foundation asked him to be a consultant on the project. Saarinen promptly declined. Letchworth quickly invited Kidd on a trip in September to meet with Eliel and his son Eero Saarinen. Saarinen agreed to be the "designing architect" and Kidd & Kidd became the principal contractors.

The Saarinens submitted plans just one month later. The exterior contours of the music hall were based on the shape of a violin! In the mid-1930s, these elegant and expansive curves were unique among the great concert halls of the world. In an enthusiastic note to Letchworth, Esther Link wrote: "…to me, the plan sings and retains the simplicity and naturalness of a raindrop." Link also insisted that two Chinese ginkgo trees from the original estate be saved. Kleinhans retains a decidedly modern look and feel even seven decades later – and the ginkgo trees still grace the grounds.

With 2,839 seats, Kleinhans ranks among the largest concert halls in the world. By comparison, Cleveland's Severance Hall seats 1,890, while Vienna's Musikverein accommodates just 1,680. Despite its size, the acoustics of the hall are extraordinary.

The Saarinens employed very precise science to achieve the desired tonal flavor, paying a great deal of attention to reverberation, diffusion and absorption. To experience how well they succeeded, take a seat in the far-upper last row in the balcony, 145 feet from center stage. Have someone sit in the middle of the stage and softly whisper "Welcome to Buffalo." The result is amazing. Every nuance of the whisper will strike your ear as though it had been secretly amplified. Every aspect of the hall, from the angles of the walls to the fabric of the seats, permits the delicate, high-pitched sibilants and subtle timbres of the phrase to travel to you without picking up spurious and competing resonances. This makes Kleinhans a superb venue for opera arias, acoustic guitar performances and violin concertos, as well as full orchestra concerts.

Under the baton of BPO maestro Franco Autori, Kleinhans Music Hall was dedicated by the Buffalo Philharmonic Orchestra in a memorable concert of Bach, Beethoven and Brahms on October 12, 1940. For Greater Buffalo and Western New York it was a night of triumph. At last, Buffalo had a truly major symphony orchestra in a truly great concert hall.

BPO concertmaster Max Miller, Music Director Franco Autori and solo harpist Laura Lambrix-Erb.

THE BUFFALO EVENING NEWS, DECEMBER 18, 1942

Handel's Messiah selections broadcast on WBEN in 1942. BPO musicians (*from left to right*) Nelson Muszinski, Carl Saxon, Max Rauchstadt, Homer Cline and Martin Danzscher.

THE BUFFALO EVENING NEWS, MAY 20, 1942

Franco Autori wearing a beret and holding a pipe, rides a bike around Buffalo, "meeting wartime conditions with a smile."

Entertains His Musicians to Prove He Can Be Human

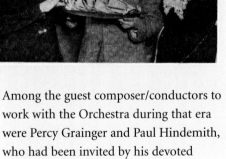

BPO ARCHIVES

Maestro Autori entertains BPO harpist Laura Lambrix-Erb (*left*) and violinist Olive Gould, at a party at his 433 Franklin Street home.

In the early 1940s, after a Saturday night concert in Kleinhans, BPO musicians and concertmaster Max Miller could be found playing jazz at Buffalo's famous Anchor Bar. The stage was improvised from an old row boat, still there today. Afterwards, everyone sampled spaghetti with Frank and Teresa's special sauce – 20 years before the world premiere of Buffalo chicken wings.

continued from page 17

Joseph Hofmann and Paul Wittgenstein. Wittgenstein had lost his right arm in the trenches of the first World War, which moved Maurice Ravel to compose his *Piano Concerto for the Left Hand*. Under Autori's baton, Wittgenstein performed the work in Kleinhans with the BPO on February 29, 1944.

IN HIS FINAL CONCERT AS MUSIC DIRECTOR, AUTORI CONDUCTED THE BUFFALO PREMIERE OF COPLAND'S *LINCOLN PORTRAIT*. NOTED AMERICAN POET CARL SANDBURG NARRATED THIS MOVING FAREWELL.

Among the guest composer/conductors to work with the Orchestra during that era were Percy Grainger and Paul Hindemith, who had been invited by his devoted student, Cameron Baird.

Buffalo's appetite for the lighter fare of Pops programming stemmed in part from the vibrant jazz scene, with legendary musicians appearing regularly in the

THE BEST AND THE MOST FOR YOUR MONEY!

Popular "POPS" Parade

with the famous

Buffalo Philharmonic Orchestra

FRED. A. RESSEL, Conducting

TONY MILITELLO *Banjo-Guitar Virtuoso*

Dancing . . . *after the concert in the large air conditioned Mary Seaton Kleinhans Room*

TUES., AUG. 1st—8:30 P. M. IN KLEINHANS MUSIC HALL

50c—70c (All Seats Reserved). Phone Lincoln 5000

Seats on sale at Philharmonic Box Office, Denton, Cottier & Daniels, Wurlitzer's and Music House.

BUFFALO PHILHARMONIC Orchestra FRANCO AUTORI Conductor

PRIMO PREMIO AL CONGRESSO INTERNAZIONALE DEI CHITARRISTI

TONY MILITELLO

Music For Everybody!

MONSTER POP CONCERT

BENEFIT OF MAINTENANCE FUND

BUFFALO PHILHARMONIC ORCHESTRA

SYLVAN LEVIN, Guest Conductor

REGINA RESNIK } Soloists
TONY MILITELLO

IN A PROGRAM OF

JEROME KERN MUSIC

SUN. EVE'G, MAY 6

MEMORIAL AUDITORIUM

All Seats Reserved; Prices $.50, $.76, $1.00

As part of the "Music for Everybody" series, this Monster Pops Concert was advertised for weeks, anticipating a full house in Memorial Auditorium.

Tonight at 7 P.M. in Delaware Park

"Sunday-in-the-Park"

Sponsored by **The Wm. Hengerer Co.** with the co-operation of the Parks Department of the City of Buffalo and the Buffalo Philharmonic Society PERFORMED BY THE HENGERER-BUFFALO PHILHARMONIC ENSEMBLE

The BPO has been performing in Delaware Park for more than 50 years! The Hengerer Co. was an early sponsor of these outdoor concerts.

Carl Sandburg

Following the bombing of Pearl Harbor in 1941, conductor André Kostelanetz commissioned three composers to produce three portraits of great Americans. Aaron Copland chose Abraham Lincoln, whose ideals he felt represented the true American spirit. A particularly poignant performance of *Lincoln Portrait* was presented at the White House for the Roosevelt Administration on July 15, 1942. Carl Sandburg narrated with Kostelantetz at the podium. Sandberg also narrated the Buffalo premiere of *Lincoln Portrait* on March 20, 1945 with Autori at the podium.

Colored Musicians Club, the Anchor Bar, the Statler Ballroom and many other area clubs. One of the Pops series known as "Music for Everybody" included a concert which featured Anne Brown.

Another souvenir from the period was the "Monster Pop Concert" on May 6, 1945. The BPO, conducted by Sylvan Levin, performed in Buffalo's brand new Memorial Auditorium to an audience of 6,271 happy patrons.

BUFFALO'S OWN TONY MILITELLO IS A FEATURED SOLOIST AT THE MONSTER POPS IN MEMORIAL AUDITORIUM.

The program featured Jerome Kern's *Mark Twain Suite* and closed with the composer's *Show Boat Scenario*. Soloists for the concert were Buffalo's own Tony Militello and Metropolitan Opera diva Regina Resnik.

During Autori's tenure in the early 1940s, music lecture series became very popular in Western New York, presented at the 20th Century Club, the Museum of Science, Buffalo Public Library and Grosvenor Library.

COURIER EXPRESS, MARCH 15, 1942

Story Teller Entrances Children

COURIER EXPRESS, MARCH 3, 1942

Stanley Travis, professor of drama at UB, narrates Prokofiev's *Peter & the Wolf* with the BPO.

Young violinist Marguerite Learning meets the famous violinist Albert Spaulding. Her teacher, Isabelle Workman Evans, is seated, (*left*). Marguerite appeared as soloist with the BPO at the age of 12.

THE BUFFALO EVENING NEWS

Carol Kimball, Nancy Lunt and Arnold Berleant look at a "Children All, Small and Tall, Come to Kleinhans Music Hall" poster.

THE BUFFALO EVENING NEWS, DECEMBER 5, 1939

School 65 pupils visit the Buffalo Consistory to hear rehearsal of the BPO and Paola Autori, wife of the conductor. (*Left to right*) Louis Schaum, James Martin and Betty Aschauer.

More than 140 youth programs were also presented, including open dress rehearsals attended by students of the Buffalo Public Schools.

Faced with growing demands as his career expanded, Autori resigned from the podium of the BPO in the spring of 1945. For his final appearance as music director on March 20, 1945, Autori conducted the Buffalo premiere of Copland's *Lincoln Portrait*. Noted American poet Carl Sandburg narrated this moving farewell.

Autori returned twice to the podium in Kleinhans, first as a guest conductor in 1970, and again in 1985, during the gala celebration of the Orchestra's 50th anniversary, when he directed the last movement of Falla's *Three Cornered Hat*.

Franco Autori passed away at age 87 in Tulsa, OK on October 16, 1990.

CHAPTER 3
THE STEINBERG YEARS

1945-1952

WILLIAM STEINBERG

BORN
August 1, 1899
Cologne, Germany

STUDIED
Piano, violin, composition, conducting

DIED
May 16, 1978
New York City, New York

FIRST BPO CONCERT
November 19, 1946
Copland - *An Outdoor Overture*
Debussy - *Prelude to the Afternoon of a Faun*
Tchaikovsky - *Symphony No.6 in B minor, op.74 "Pathetique"*
Strauss, R. - *Til Eulenspiegel's Merry Pranks*

LAST CONCERT AS MUSIC DIRECTOR
March 30, April 1, 1952
Verdi - *Te Deum*
    Cameron Baird, guest conductor
Mahler - *Symphony No.2 in C minor "Resurrection"*
    Ruth Johnson, soprano
    Panna Genia, soprano
    Nell Tangeman, mezzo-soprano

RETURN BPO ENGAGEMENT
March 13 & 15, 1977

UB LIBRARY ARCHIVES (PERRY COLLECTION)

BUFFALO HIGHLIGHTS
- Added 22 new musicians in 1946 including several emigres from postwar Europe
- NBC Radio Broadcasts 1947-1949
- First commercial BPO recording in October, 1947: Shostakovich, *Symphony No. 7*

CAREER HIGHLIGHTS
- Succeeded Otto Klemperer as principal conductor, Cologne Opera, 1924
- Maestro, Frankfurt Opera, 1929
- Emigrated to Palestine, 1936
- Founded Israel Philharmonic with Bronislav Hubermann
- Music Director, Boston Symphony Orchestra, 1969-1972
- Recorded with Jascha Heifetz, Nathan Milstein and Vladimir Horowitz
- Composed cantata for soloists, chorus and orchestra at age 13
- Conducted the sound track for the MGM film *Song of Love*, starring Katherine Hepburn
- Conducted world premiere of Copland's *Billy the Kid*

"I prefer working with a young orchestra which I hope to develop into America's greatest."

- WILLIAM STEINBERG, WHEN ASKED WHY HE CHOSE THE BUFFALO PHILHARMONIC ORCHESTRA OVER SEVERAL OTHERS

THE STEINBERG YEARS

1945-1952

BPO MUSICIANS 1945-1946

VIOLIN I
Max Miller, Concertmaster
Louis Podgorski
Karol Barabasz
Hans Hagen
Albert Koch
George Kogler
Wallace Michalski
Paul Muni
Oswald Rantucci
Ivan Shapiro
Ann Slick
Harry Slick
Theodore Stanley
Matthew Tworek

VIOLIN II
Igor Prince
Andrew Dengos
George Elflein
Jan Geerts
Erich Hechter
Eva Landsberger

Arthur Lundequist
Walter Raszeja
Stavros Theodore
Charles Termini

VIOLA
Fred A. Ressel
Cornelius Boulange
Edward Gerstel
Pauline Kappler
Dorthea Kelly
Harold Nissenson
Oscar Witte
William Zacharias

CELLO
Rudolf Doblin
Nicholas D'Addio
William Fahlbusch
Erna Field
Raymond Frey
Lucille D'Addio Greco
Frank McGoldrick

William Schmidt
Thomas Sicurella

STRING BASS
Martin Danzscher
Homer Cline
Jerome Contino
Nelson Muczynski
Max Rauschstadt
John Wade

FLUTE
Eric Evans
José Acosta
Louis Cheskin

PICCOLO
José Acosta

OBOE
Mark Lifshey
Walter Kessler
Ezra Kotzin

ENGLISH HORN
Walter Kessler

CLARINET
Wallace Shapiro
Theodore Buczek

BASS CLARINET
William Nassal

CONTRABASSOON
William G. Wisler
Herbert Reich

FRENCH HORN
Ginesio Lecce
Herbert J. Flumerfeldt
Fred Holcomb
Charles H. Jepson

TRUMPET
Louis Impellieter
Eugene Bishop
Laurence Getchell

TROMBONE
Angelo Tulumello
Santolo Carriero
Albert Demske

TUBA
Isidor Termini

TIMPANI
August Stoerr

PERCUSSION
Edward Adams
Edmund Oroschin

HARP
Martha Gomph

PIANO/CELESTE
Beth Bowman Wolanek

NOTABLE GUEST CONDUCTORS

Igor Stravinsky, composer, guest conductor | January 21, 1947

Howard Hanson, guest conductor | February 17, 1948

Leonard Bernstein, conductor, pianist | January 18, 1949

Virgil Thomson, composer, conductor | March 1, 1949

Dimitri Mitropoulos, guest conductor | February 4 & 6, 1951

Heitor Villa-Lobos, composer, conductor | February 3 & 5, 1952

NOTABLE GUEST SOLOISTS

Zino Francescatti, violinist | January 8, 1946

Regina Resnik, soprano | February 5, 1946

Nathan Milstein, violinist | March 19, 1946 | December 16 & 18, 1951

Jasha Heifetz, violinist | February 11, 1947

Rudolf Serkin, pianist | April 1, 1947

Vladimir Horowitz, pianist | March 2, 1948

Zino Francescatti, violinist | March 16, 1948

Jan Peerce, tenor | December 7, 1948

Nathan Milstein, violinist | February 1, 1949

Artur Rubinstein, pianist | February 15, 1949 | March 16 & 18, 1952

Margaret Truman, soprano | November 13 & 15, 1949

Zara Nelsova, cellist | November 27 & 29, 1949

Gary Graffman, pianist | February 5 & 7, 1950

Isaac Stern, violinist | November 5 & 7, 1950

Joseph Szigeti, violinist | December 3 & 5, 1950

Eugene Istomin, pianist | December 17 & 19, 1950

Alexander Schneider, violinist | December 2 & 4, 1951

Milton Katims, violinist | December 2 & 4, 1951

Frank Miller, cellist | December 2 & 4, 1951

Mieczyslaw Horszowski, pianist | December 2 & 4, 1951

Paul Tortelier, cellist | March 2 & 4, 1952

Benny Goodman, clarinetist | November 15 & 16, 1952

CHAIRMEN OF THE BPO BOARD OF DIRECTORS

1944-1946 Mr. James How

1947-1950 Mr. Frank N. Farrar

1951-1952 Mr. Charles H. Augspurger

THE STEINBERG YEARS

1945-1952

Once World War II came to a close, the nation quickly rebounded. Families were reunited and new families were started. This made housing scarce. When Benny Goodman gave benefit concerts, he asked citizens to pledge rooms for rent for returning GIs instead of donating money! The 33 rpm LP had just been invented and Americans were buying 100,000 television sets each week.

The time was prime for a new maestro in the revered opera-symphonic tradition.

After the Nazi regime forced his resignation from his conducting post in Frankfurt, William Steinberg formed what is now the Israel Philharmonic in Tel Aviv. Shortly thereafter he met Arturo Toscanini, who invited the young maestro to become the associate conductor of the NBC Symphony Orchestra in New York City, where he served from 1938 through 1941. After a variety of guest appearances in the U.S. during the war, Steinberg was named permanent guest conductor of the San Francisco Opera in 1944. It was Toscanini who

William Steinberg (*left*) conducts a BPO rehearsal. (*Right*) Arturo Toscanini, conductor of the NBC Orchestra in New York, invited the young Steinberg to become the associate conductor of the NBC Symphony Orchestra, where he served from 1938 through 1941.

suggested to Cameron Baird that William Steinberg might be the perfect music director for the BPO. A major coup was achieved when Baird succeeded in bringing Steinberg to Buffalo.

For his first concert at the opening of the 1945-1946 season, the BPO's new maestro offered a program of Bach, Beethoven, Strauss and Sibelius, topped off by Ravel's *Bolero*. It was a sign that William Steinberg understood very well that serious offerings could be served up with a lighter touch.

During his seven-season tenure as music director of the Buffalo Philharmonic, Steinberg raised the BPO's performance level and expanded

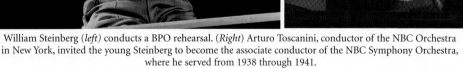

MATT TWOREK

BPO violinists Max Miller, Paul Muni and Matt Tworek. Miller joined WBEN as music director, bringing Muni and Tworek with him to the WBEN Orchestra, which played live as part of the programming. Many BPO musicians moonlighted to augment their income.

The tone and tempo of the Pops concerts was lighthearted. A delightful story is recalled by long-term BPO violinist Matt Tworek, now in his 90s.

"I liked to play gypsy fiddle tunes at a little restaurant near Kleinhans Music Hall. I would stroll among the tables of patrons on Saturday nights before a BPO concert. I loved the music, plus it gave me a little pocket change. On one occasion I remember, it was February 1947 at Kleinhans, I was called to Mr. Steinberg's dressing room during intermission. Oh boy, everybody was chiming in as if I was in really big trouble. Even I was a little scared when I entered his room. The maestro smiled and just wanted me to know that he and his dinner guest really enjoyed my fiddle playing the previous night. That guest was Jascha Heifetz."

Anne Brown was the original "Bess" in *Porgy and Bess*, selected by Gershwin during a private audition in his New York apartment in 1924. She appeared several times with the BPO over the years.

To Play Here March 4

Menahem Pressler debuted in America with the BPO at the age of 17, on March 4, 1947. His career would extend over five decades, most notably since 1955 as pianist with the Beaux Arts Trio.

Benny Goodman on the clarinet playing with the BPO in All High Stadium in July, 1947, Ralph Black conducting. An appreciative audience applauds.

the Orchestra. He welcomed with open arms the influx of talented musicians among the many immigrants who, like Steinberg himself, sought new lives and careers in the U.S. after the war. Their presence on stage, primarily in the strings, resulted in the distinctly European sound which began to resonate from the BPO during that period. To this was added Steinberg's relentless demand for impeccable performance.

The tone and timbre of the Orchestra is well-preserved through the recorded broadcasts the BPO made on the NBC national radio network in 1947 and 1949, now in the Library of Congress.

RECORDINGS OF BPO BROADCASTS ON NBC RADIO IN 1947 AND 1949 ARE IN THE LIBRARY OF CONGRESS.

Stellar performances of Beethoven's Symphony No.6, Debussy's *Prelude to the Afternoon of a Faun* and Richard Strauss' *Till Eulenspiegel's Merry Pranks*, among others, were recorded.

Steinberg conducted the Orchestra's very first commercial recording. The *"Leningrad"* Symphony No.7, by Dmitri Shostakovich was released in 1947 on the Musicraft label (now available on CD).

In 1949, the BPO embarked on its very first documented tour. The itinerary included Pennsylvania, New York and several New England states.

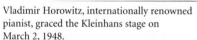

Vladimir Horowitz, internationally renowned pianist, graced the Kleinhans stage on March 2, 1948.

Morton Gould, composer, conductor, arranger, and pianist.

Zino Francescatti plays the Paganini Concerto on January 8, 1946 on his 1727 Hart Stradivarius violin.

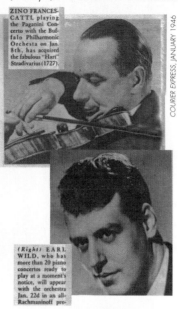

ZINO FRANCESCATTI, playing the Paganini Concerto with the Buffalo Philharmonic Orchestra on Jan. 8th, has acquired the fabulous "Hart" Stradivarius (1727).

(Right) EARL WILD, who has more than 20 piano concertos ready to play at a moment's notice, will appear with the orchestra Jan. 22d in an all-Rachmaninoff pro-

Earl Wild appeared with the BPO under Steinberg on January 22, 1946, performing an all-Rachmaninoff program.

A wealth of important soloists added grace and pizzazz to the Philharmonic seasons during the Steinberg years. Among many others were pianists Vladimir Horowitz, Artur Rubinstein and Rudolf Serkin, and violinists Jascha Heifetz, Zino Francescatti and Nathan Milstein. Stars from the world of opera included soprano Anne Brown, soprano Margaret Truman (the President's daughter) and Metropolitan tenor John Priebe.

Notable composer/conductor appearances during that period included Igor Stravinsky, who presented an

Steinberg samples one of his favorite dishes, Viennese plum dumplings prepared by his wife, for an article by Alice Partridge, the *Courier Express* food editor.

all-Russian program, including his suites from *Petrouchka* and *Firebird*, and the young and flamboyant Leonard Bernstein, who conducted the BPO in performances of Mozart and Brahms, as well as switch-hitting as conductor/soloist from the keyboard in Ravel's zesty Concerto in G.

Delightful family, Pops and youth concert programs were offered, primarily under the baton of assistant conductors Rudolf Doblin and Henry Aaron. By 1950, the value of youth concerts was recognized by the Buffalo Public School System. A 74-page syllabus for

Among many refinements in the design of Kleinhans Music Hall were plans for a modest pipe organ. Unbeknownst to many, a large center panel of the back wall facing the audience can be electrically lifted into a recess in the ceiling, revealing an area just large enough to accommodate the pipes of a chapel organ, with the longer bass pipes lying horizontally, as shown in the photo.

More than a decade after Kleinhans was completed, a pipe organ was finally installed, just in time for a performance of Bach's B minor Mass on December 12, 1950, conducted by William Steinberg, with the Schola Cantorum and the Buffalo Oratorio Chorus, Cameron Baird, director.

Built by the renowned Schlicker Organ Company of Tonawanda, it was installed on loan, and removed after the debut performance. About two years later, a full-register modern electric organ was permanently installed in Kleinhans.

continued on page 31

THE FIRST RECORDING

THE BPO ON LP AND ON THE AIR

Although the BPO was heard on many local radio broadcasts during the early years, it was more than a decade before the first recording took place.

The 1946 recording of Shostakovich's Symphony No.7 *"Leningrad"* by the BPO under William Steinberg's baton focused international attention on the orchestra and represents two important firsts. Not only had the Shostakovich symphony never before been recorded, this was also the first recording made in Kleinhans Music Hall.

How did Steinberg choose Shostakovich's symphony for this landmark recording? A charming tale tells of a chance meeting on a train to Moscow in 1932, when Steinberg was 33 and Shostakovich just 26 years old. Fourteen years later, when Steinberg requested permission to record the Shostakovich's Symphony No.7 *"Leningrad"* in Buffalo, the composer cabled a quick consent.

Produced near the end of the 78 rpm format, the 75-minute composition was recorded in four-minute "takes," each of which made one side of a record, and the recording was issued on a set of eight disks on the Musicraft label. The first album was air mailed to Shostakovich.

Steinberg also put the BPO in the limelight nationally with a series of broadcasts on the NBC radio network in 1947 and 1949. The original master tapes of these programs are now held by the Library of Congress.

THE BUFFALO EVENING NEWS, DECEMBER 4, 1946

December 4, 1946

CHANCE MEETING LEADS TO RECORDING OF RED SYMPHONY

Picture on the Picture Page.

By MILDRED SPENCER

Because of the chance meeting of two musicians on a Moscow-bound train 14 years ago, the Buffalo Philharmonic Orchestra this morning made the first recording of Dimitri Shostakovich's Seventh Symphony.

Conductor William Steinberg was traveling to Moscow to conduct Gustav Mahler's Seventh Symphony in 1932 when a porter approached him to ask if he would talk to a young musician who admired him very much. The musician was Mr. Shostakovich.

Although the two have never met since that time, when they sat up all night discussing music, their admiration for each other's work has continued. When the question of recording the Seventh Symphony arose, Mr. Shostakovich cabled permission for Mr. Steinberg and the Buffalo Philharmonic to do the job exclusively.

"Clam" Is Dreaded

The 75-minute composition, sometimes called the "most-discussed symphony of the century," was recorded by Musicraft Records Inc. in 4-minute "takes," each of which makes one side of a record. The first album will be sent air-mail to Shostakovich next week.

"It's a real job," the perspiring, shirt-sleeved conductor admitted during an interval between records. "Even the slightest error—'clam,' the recorders call it—spoils everything."

Mr. Steinberg stopped the orchestra several times to repeat

Russian composer Dimitri Shostakovich

THE NEW YORK TIMES, OCTOBER 26, 1947

BPO ARCHIVES

WILLIAM STEINBERG
Shostakovich—Symphony No. 7 "Leningrad"

William Steinberg
ORCHESTRE PHILHARMONIQUE DE BUFFALO
EARLY NORTH AMERICAN ORCHESTRA RECORDINGS

DIMITRI SHOSTAKOVITCH
SYMPHONIE N. 7 DE 60 'LENINGRAD'
ENREGISTRÉE EN DÉCEMBRE 1946
PREMIER ENREGISTREMENT MONDIAL
WORLD PREMIERE RECORDING

BPO ARCHIVES

Recordings are often re-released in a newer format when the market warrants. The original 78 (not shown) of the BPO's first recording, Dimitri Shostakovich's Symphony No.7 *"Leningrad"* under the baton of William Steinberg, was re-released onto an LP, then re-released again on CD.

COURIER EXPRESS, DECEMBER 5, 1946

Musicraft engineers and BPO management examine the equipment to be used to record the BPO.

Radio broadcasts were also an important way to hear the BPO. Maestro Steinberg and BPO Manager Robert F. MacIntyre help a WHLD (Niagara Falls, NY) radio station representative correct the radio pickup for volume in preparation for a broadcast.

Smilin' Bob Smith was an MC and Bison quizmaster for WBEN Radio. He is perhaps better known as Buffalo Bob Smith, host of the "Howdy Doody Show," which entertained youngsters and adults alike across the nation from 1947 to 1960.

Orchestra Groups Lined Up For Quiz of Two Cities Sunday

By JIM TRANTER

A pair of dream teams have been lined up for the Quiz of Two Cities this Sunday at 4:30 over WBEN. Get this: Guy Fraser Harrison, conductor of the Rochester Civic Orchestra, leads the Rochester group and Rudolph Dobbin, pinch-hitting for William Steinberg as conductor of the Buffalo Philharmonic, will head the local contingent. Smilin' Bob Smith, genial emcee and Bison quizmaster, will steer his

The quiz contest will follow half-hour concert by the Buffalo Philharmonic, to be broadcast 4 over WBEN and marking t opening of a fund-raising dri So if you want a full Sunday aft noon of entertainment, head the Erlanger Theater and listen the broadcast by the Philharmo and stay right there for the Q of Two Cities. There are no tick and everybody's welcome.

Bob Smith

Thirty members of the BPO, under the baton of Victor Alessandro, conductor of the Oklahoma City Symphony Orchestra, entertain young polio patients at Children's Hospital in 1946.

Margaret Mott, head of the Grosvenor Library Music Department, Mr. and Mrs. Cameron Baird and William Steinberg. Good friends following a concert are captured by a *Buffalo Evening News* photographer.

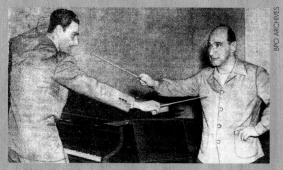

THE BATON

Gus Farrell, conductor of the Swing Band, and William Steinberg face off with dueling batons! Steinberg conducted the composers as written, while Farrell performed the same compositions in swing tempo in "Classics vs. Swing – the Battle of the Century" in January 1948, a light-hearted chapter in the long standing feud between the classics and popular music.

The baton came into fashion during the 1720s. During the Renaissance, some conductors thumped a long walking staff on the floor, but generally conductors simply stamped a foot. That is, until French composer Jean-Baptiste Lully (1632-1687) died from complications after piercing his foot during a performance. Waving a wand by hand seemed much safer, and thus the tradition took hold. Modern maestros usually make practical choices on what to wave. Steinberg's baton was very long (he was quite short), while Michael Tilson Thomas' baton is short (he is rather tall). Doc Severinsen has been known to use a soup ladle for fun and Franco Autori was known to use a knitting needle. In a pinch, everyone simply uses a pencil.

teachers was created by educators and BPO staff in preparation for Philharmonic education concerts.

WBEN radio's "An Evening of Familiar Music" in the 1940s was just one of the ways in which the BPO provided Buffalo with lighter music. "Classics vs. Swing – the Battle of the Century" was also a big hit in January 1948, followed by dancing in the Mary Seaton Room.

To launch the 1946 BPO fundraising campaign, WBEN Radio hosted the Quiz of Two Cities. What was a bit unusual, in retrospect, was not the fundraiser

WITHIN THE YEAR, SMILIN' BOB SMITH WOULD BECOME BUFFALO BOB SMITH WITH HIS SIDEKICK, HOWDY DOODY.

itself, but the host, Smilin' Bob Smith. Within the year, Smilin' Bob would become Buffalo Bob Smith with his sidekick, Howdy Doody, on the nationally televised "Howdy Doody Show." Who knows? Perhaps his *pro bono* appearance on behalf of the BPO helped launch this local boy into the national limelight.

Steinberg's success in Buffalo sparked the remainder of his exceptional career. It also allowed the BPO to be highly selective in choosing his successor. Two years were spent searching for the ideal music director.

INTERMEZZO

Music director of the Columbus Philharmonic Orchestra until 1949, Izler Solomon served as BPO conductor-in-residence 1952-1953.
PHOTOGRAPH FROM PHOTOGRAPHERSDIRECT.COM

Milton Katims, associate conductor of the NBC Orchestra.
PHOTOGRAPH BY JOSEF SCAYLEA, FROM MOHAI AND HISTORYLINK.ORG

Leopold Stokowski, former conductor of the Philadelphia Orchestra.
PHOTO FROM BRIGHTCECILIA.COM

Joseph Rosenstock, general director of the New York City Opera Company.
PHOTOGRAPH BY LOUIS MELANCON, METROPOLITAN OPERA INTERNATIONAL RADIO BROADCAST INFORMATION CENTER

Josef Krips, music director of the London Symphony Orchestra.
BPO ARCHIVES

Otto Klemperer, conductor of the Philharmonia in London, recording for EMI.
J. WARREN PERRY COLLECTION, UNIVERSITY AT BUFFALO

Efrem Kurtz, music director of the Houston Symphony Orchestra.
PHOTOGRAPH FROM WDR3.DE

André Kostelanetz, best known for conducting "easy listening" music for Columbia Records.
PHOTOGRAPH FROM THE ESTATE OF ANDRÉ KOSTELANETZ

Season's Conductors of Buffalo Philharmonic Orchestra

Six of the renowned guest conductors during the BPO's "Intermezzo" seasons are depicted in caricature by artist Stu Hample in *The Buffalo Evening News* on October 22, 1952. (*From left to right*) Joseph Rostenstock, Izler Solomon, Milton Katims, Leopold Stowkowski, Josef Krips and William Steinberg.

THE BUFFALO EVENING NEWS, OCTOBER 22, 1952

The early 1950s was a post-Korean War era of change. Businesses turned from making weapons to building new homes and cars. The national economy was booming and public attitudes were upbeat. Thousands of veterans returned to school to earn college degrees on the GI Bill of Rights. Families were started and schools were constructed. Education took center stage and music played a role.

Buffalo's future seemed unlimited. Roswell Park Memorial Institute was under construction and Veteran's Hospital was dedicated to the legacy of national heroes. But just below the surface, an insidious economic decline was taking place. Although Buffalo still ranked sixth in the nation in steel production in 1950, the move of aircraft manufacturer Curtiss-Wright from Buffalo to Ohio in 1946 marked the beginning of an industrial exodus that would continue unabated for decades. In 1952, DuPont followed Curtiss-Wright to Ohio, and Allied Chemical relocated to Virginia. Even the beer industry became a battle ground. National companies successfully undercut local Buffalo breweries, putting one by one out of business.

In the world of music, however, the Buffalo Philharmonic had emerged as a player on the international scene. The remarkable maturity the BPO achieved under the baton of William Steinberg generated a deluge of inquiries from conductors around the world who wished to succeed him on the podium. The BPO Society named Izler Solomon "conductor-in-residence" and took its time searching for just the right new maestro for the Orchestra.

The illustrious lineup of guest conductors, all of whom were keen to direct a fine orchestra within the already celebrated walls of Kleinhans Music Hall, might almost have been auditioning for the post.

February 15, 1952, telegram from Dimitri Mitropolus, renowned conductor, to Cameron Baird, congratulating the BPO on the choice of Izler Solomon as conductor-in-residence.

WESTERN UNION

BUB241 PD=NEWYORK NY 15 1230P=
CAMERON BAIRD=
BFLO PHILHARMONIC ORCHESTRA=1069 DELAWARE =
PLEASE ALLOW ME TO CONGRATULATE YOU ON YOUR EXCELLENT CHOI
I CONSIDER IZLER SOLOMON ONE OF THE MOST COMPETENT
CONDUCTORS BECAUSE OF HIS BACKGROUND SERIOUS MIND AND
EXCELLENT MUSICIANSHIP=
D MITROPOLUS =

Pianist Eugene Istomin performed the Chopin Piano Concerto No.2 in December 1952.

Ballerina Melissa Hayden performed with the Ballet Theater under the direction of Joseph Levine in January 1954.

Benny Goodman performed Copland's Clarinet Concerto on Opening Night of the 1952-53 season, one of many performances with the BPO.

Violinist Jascha Heifetz performed Beethoven's Violin Concerto in A major under the baton of Josef Krips in 1954.

Mezzo-soprano Rise Stevens performed works of Mozart and Gluck under the baton of Josef Krips.

Hollywood pianist Oscar Levant performed Gershwin Piano Concerto in F major under the baton of Izler Solomon.

Pianist William Kapell, who championed new works, performed Rachmaninoff's Piano Concerto No.3 with Rosenstock at the podium in February 1953.

Famed violinist Yehudi Menuhin performed the Bruch Violin Concerto No.1 in G major under the baton of Milton Katims in November 1952.

The Budapest Quartet performed the Martinů Concerto for String Quartet and Orchestra in March 1953.

Milton Katims guest conducted in December, 1952, followed by Leopold Stokowski in January 1953, and Joseph Rosenstock in February. Josef Krips guest conducted in both February and March, and Buffalo's own Cameron Baird conducted the Buffalo Schola Cantorum on March 26. Otto Klemperer wielded the baton in November 1953, followed on the podium by Efrem Kurtz in December. Joseph Rosenstock conducted in January 1954, followed by André Kostelanetz in February. Both Katims and Krips came back in the spring of 1954, Krips conducting no fewer than three programs.

Under these experts batons played a host of renowned classical soloists including violinists Yehudi Menuhin and Jascha Heifetz, pianists Eugene Istomin and William Kapell, and mezzo-soprano Rise Stevens. Hollywood stars like Oscar Levant and jazz great Benny Goodman performed under Solomon's baton.

Izler Solomon presided over this procession of extraordinary talent. Solomon came to Buffalo from Ohio, where he served as Music Director of the Columbus Philharmonic Orchestra throughout the 1940s. He was a champion of 20th century American music. As conductor of the Illinois Symphony Orchestra, he introduced more than 150 American works.

Ralph Black was BPO manager during this period. Black may be best remembered for starting a project called "Music USA" which celebrated the contributions of community orchestras across the nation, with an emphasis on Western New York. Local conductors of satellite orchestras around Buffalo were invited to conduct the BPO in programs of regional content, somewhat reminiscent of the early ERB programming during the Depression years.

In this same, local vein, the D'Youville College Women's Chorus under the direction of Gertrude Lutzi, and the Canisius College Men's Chorus under Robert Schultz, jointly performed *The Marriage of Figaro* with the BPO in January 1953. And the BPO maintained a busy schedule of youth concerts, most of which brought students into the impressive Kleinhans Music Hall.

One of the guest conductors who stood out among the candidates for the BPO podium was Josef Krips, the esteemed maestro of the Vienna State Opera and the London Symphony. His appointment as music director was announced in the March 1953 program, concluding the drama of the BPO's maestro intermezzo.

The appointment of Josef Krips as Conductor and Musical Director is proudly announced.

NOTABLE GUEST CONDUCTORS

Milton Katims, guest conductor | November 30 & December 2, 14 & 16, 1952 | February 14 & 16, 1954

Leopold Stokowski, guest conductor | January 18 & 20, 1953

Joseph Rosenstock, guest conductor | February 1 & 3, 1953

Josef Krips, guest conductor | February 15, 17, 23 and 28, 1953 | March 1 & 3, 1953

Cameron Baird, director | March 26, 1953

William Steinberg, conductor | March 26, 1953

Otto Klemperer, guest conductor | November 15 & 17, 1953

Efrem Kurtz, guest conductor November 29 & December 1, 13 & 15, 1953

André Kostelanetz, guest conductor | January 31 & February 2, 1954

NOTABLE GUEST SOLOISTS

Benny Goodman, clarinetist | November 15 & 16, 1952

Yehudi Menuhin, violinist | November 30 & December 2, 1952

Eugene Istomin, pianist | December 14 &16, 1952

William Kapell, pianist | February 1 & 3, 1953

Rise Stevens, mezzo-soprano | February 15 & 17, 1953

Budapest Quartet | March 1 & 3, 1953

Oscar Levant, pianist | March 15 & 17, 1953

Winifred Cecil, soprano | March 29 & 31, 1953

Michael Rabin, violinist | November 15 & 17, 1953

Theodore Lettvin, pianist | December 13 & 15, 1953

Melissa Hayden, ballerina | January 3, 1954

Paul Badura-Skoda, pianist | January 31 &, February 2, 1954

Jascha Heifetz, violinist | February 28 & March 2, 1954

Alexander Schneider, violinist | March 7, 1954

Paul Tortelier, cellist | March 7, 1954

Mieczyslaw Horszowski, pianist | March 7, 1954

Ines Carrillo, pianist | March 14 & 16, 1945

CHAIRMEN OF THE BPO BOARD OF DIRECTORS

1951-1952 Mr. Charles H. Augspurger

1953-1954 Mr. Edward H. Kavinoky

34

THE KRIPS YEARS

1954-1963

JOSEF KRIPS

BORN
April 8, 1902
Vienna, Austria

STUDIED
Violin

DIED
October 13, 1974
Geneva, Switzerland

FIRST BPO CONCERT
February 15 & 17, 1953 (guest conductor)
Mozart - Symphony No.41 in C major,
K.551 *"Jupiter"*

Mozart - *The Marriage of Figaro:*
Non so piu cosa son

Mozart - *The Marriage of Figaro:*
Voi che sapete

Gluck - *Orfeo ed Euridice:*
Che faro senza, Euridice
    Rise Stevens, mezzo-soprano

Schubert - Symphony No.7 in C major

LAST CONCERT AS MUSIC DIRECTOR
May 1, 1963
Beethoven - *Leonore* Overture No.3, op.72
Beethoven - Symphony No.9 in D minor,
op.125 *"Chorale"*
    Joanna Simon, contralto
    Mallory Walker, tenor
    Yi-Kwei Sze, bass/baritone
    Buffalo Schola Cantorum,
        Richard Sheil, director
    Guido Chorus,
        Clyde D. Kline, director

J. WARREN PERRY COLLECTION, UNIVERSITY AT BUFFALO

RETURN BPO ENGAGEMENTS
February 8-10, 1970

BUFFALO HIGHLIGHTS
- Led BPO tours of the eastern United States and Canada
- 25th Anniversary Program featuring Glenn Gould as soloist in Beethoven's *"Emperor"* Concerto
- Symphony Circle was named

CAREER HIGHLIGHTS
- Resident Conductor, Vienna Staatsoper, 1933-1938
- Conducted *Don Giovanni* at the 1946 Salzburg Festival reopening
- Principal Conductor, London Symphony Orchestra, 1950-1954
- Music Director, San Francisco Symphony, 1963-1970

"Mozart is, of all composers, the most difficult to conduct and I can tell you why: two bars and you are suddenly transported to Heaven. It is very hard to keep your bearings when you are there."

- JOSEF KRIPS

CHAPTER 5
THE KRIPS YEARS
1954-1963

BPO MUSICIANS 1954-1955

VIOLIN I
Max Miller, Concertmaster
Harry Taub
Willy Frey
Karol Barabasz
Louis Podgorski
Laszlo Hajos
Igor Prince
Maximilian Huttner
Joan Macdonald
Oswald Rantucci
Deryck Aird
Joseph Romano
Loretta Reed
Philip Teibel
Rivka Mandelkern
Eugene Kaza

VIOLIN II
Bernard Mandelkern
Julius Kovach
Meyer Balsom
Eva Black

Lois Murray
Sylvia Davis
Harry Slick
Ann Slick
Irena Helinski
Andrew Dengos
Kurt Brychta
Charles Termini

VIOLA
Fred Ressel
Edward Gerstel
Aaron Juvelier
Mimi Denton
Harold Nissenson
Benjamin Stolow
Ivan Shapiro
Arthur Welte
William Zacharias

CELLO
Analee Camp
Dodia Feldin
Mary Vaughan
William Fahlbusch
Dorthea Jump
Dimitri Carapetyan
Alfreds Ozolin
Thomas Sicurella

STRING BASS
Theodor Mayer
Edward Mandel
Martin Danzscher
Frank Primerano
Homer Cline
Nelson Muszynski
Erling Alfee

FLUTE
Donald Macdonald
Jean Harling
Christine Nazzi

PICCOLO
Jean Harling

OBOE
Roger Roller
Herbert Resnick
Rene Corne

ENGLISH HORN
Rene Corne

CLARINET
Allen Sigel
Raymond Fiutak
Anthony Gilio

BASS CLARINET
Anthony Gilio

BASSOON
Ivan Diachun
Herbert Turrentine
William Wisler

CONTRABASSOON
William Wisler

FRENCH HORN
Ginesio Lecce
Fred Holcomb
Elissa Nassy
Barbara Bloomer

TRUMPET
Alex Wilson
Peter Crino
Eugene Bishop

TROMBONE
Philip Laspina
Albert Demske
Edwin Roman

BASS TROMBONE
Edwin Roman

TUBA
William Montieth

TIMPANI
George D'Anna

PERCUSSION
August Stoerr
John Rowland

HARP
Phyllis Hastings

LIBRARIAN
Oscar Witte

PERSONNEL MANAGER
Eugene Bishop

NOTABLE GUEST CONDUCTORS

Pierre Monteux, guest conductor | January 14 & 15, 1956 and December 16 & 18, 1956
Arthur Fiedler, guest conductor | January 19 & 20, 1961

NOTABLE GUEST SOLOISTS

Rise Stevens, mezzo-soprano | February 15 & 17, 1953
Jascha Heifetz, violinist | February 28 and March 2, 1954
Mieczyslaw Horszowski, pianist | March 7, 1954
Isaac Stern, violinist | January 30 &, 1 February 1955
Van Cliburn, pianist | February 27 & 1 March, 1955
Nell Rankin, mezzo-soprano | March 27 & 29, 1955
Robert Casadesus, pianist | November 20 & 22, 1955
Nathan Milstein, violinist | January 29 & 31, 1956
Artur Rubinstein, pianist | March 4 & 6, 1956
Gregor Piatigorsky, cellist | March 25 & 27, 1956
Clifford Curzon, pianist | December 2 & 4, 1956
Zino Francescatti, violinist | February 3 & 5, 1957
Yehudi Menuhin, violinist | November 3 & 5, 1957
Pierre Fournier, cellist | December 1, 1957
Yi-Kwei Sze, bass-baritone | February 16 & 18, 1958
Gaby Casadesus, pianist | November 2 & 4, 1958
Gary Graffman, pianist | November 30 & December 2, 1958

Andres Segovia, guitarist | March 1 & 3, 1959
Mischa Elman, violinist | April 5 & 7, 1959
Leonard Pennario, pianist | November 1 & 3, 1959
Eudice Shapiro, violinist | November 15 & 17, 1959
John Browning, pianist | November 29 & December 1, 1959
Witold Malcuzynski, pianist | January 17 & 19, 1960
Henryk Szeryng, violinist | March 13 &, 15, 1960
Glenn Gould, pianist | November 6 & 8, 1960
Victoria de Los Angeles, soprano | April 2 & 4, 1961
Philippe Entremont, pianist | November 5 & 7, 1961
Claudio Arrau, pianist | January 7 & 9, 1962
Michael Rabin, violinist | January 21 & 23, 1962
Jaime Laredo, violinist | April 1 & 3, 1962
Jorge Bolet, pianist | December 2 & 4, 1962
Byron Janis, pianist | January 20 & 22, 1963
Erica Morini, violinist | February 17 & 19, 1963
Roberta Peters, soprano | April 28 & 30, 1963

CHAIRMEN OF THE BPO BOARD OF DIRECTORS

1953-1954 Mr. Edward H. Kavinoky
1955 Mr. Dudley M. Irwin
1956-1958 Mr. Robert I. Millonzi
1960 -1961 Mr. Franz T. Stone
1962-1963 Mr. David J. Laub

THE KRIPS YEARS
1954-1963

The Salk polio vaccine became available in 1955, and the Russians launched Sputnik in 1957. Television was taking over; the networks were expanding and talk shows like the "Today Show" and the "Tonight Show" were changing the patterns of family life, while programs like "Leave It to Beaver" extolled them. Beneath the halcyon veneer of the 1950s, however, a battle was brewing. In 1954, the Brown v. Board of Education ruling sparked what would come to be known as the civil rights movement. Rosa Parks refused to give up her seat on the bus in 1955, and Martin Luther King, Jr. was arrested in 1962. The rise of the Queen City's suburbs left the inner city to dwindle. While the South was reluctantly moving toward integration, Buffalo was rapidly sprawling into segregation.

Into this milieu stepped Josef Krips, the refined maestro of the London Symphony. First Conductor of the Vienna State Opera (*Staatsoper*) before World War II, Krips spent the tumultuous war years working in a factory, emerging to resurrect the *Staatsoper* as well as the Vienna Philharmonic and the Salzburg Festival. His reputation for building orchestras led him to the helm of the London Symphony in 1949, from whence he was wooed to Buffalo, first as guest conductor in February 1953, when he is said to have fallen in love with Kleinhans Music Hall, both visually and acoustically. The opportunity to work with the remarkable musical talent

J. WARREN PERRY COLLECTION, UNIVERSITY AT BUFFALO

Krips' instrument was the violin. Also a fine pianist, at 19 he was appointed rehearsal conductor for a chorus under Felix Weingartner.

developed by Steinberg and a very warm reception in Buffalo combined to clinch the deal. With such impeccable credentials, Krips' appointment as music director of the Buffalo Philharmonic was met with considerable international notice.

Although still officially with the London Symphony for a full year following his appointment as BPO music director in March 1953, maestro Krips managed to conduct a full cycle of all nine Beethoven symphonies in Buffalo in the spring of 1954.

Under Krips, the BPO expanded yet again. The orchestra's season was extended and new players were hired. Vacant chairs were filled by an audition process

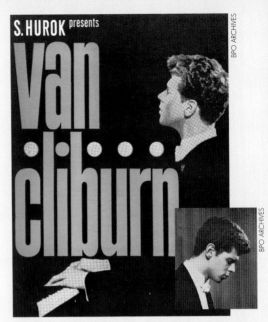

S. HUROK presents

van cliburn

Van Cliburn was a guest soloist with the BPO at the age of 20. The young pianist would win the International Tchaikovsky Competition just three years later. Over the course of his meteoric career, Van Cliburn performed many times with the BPO, most recently with JoAnn Falletta in 2007.

Artur Rubinstein Will Appear In Buffalo and Lockport Concerts

Artur Rubinstein performed the Beethoven Piano Concerto No.4 with the BPO in March 1956.

THE NBC LIBRARY
ARTURO TOSCANINI CONDUCTOR

The Philharmonic Society presents the NBC/Toscanini orchestral collection to the Buffalo & Erie County Public Library. Scores and parts will be borrowed by the BPO as well as by local orchestras. (*From left to right*) Society women's committee president Mrs. John F. Huber, Jr., library board chairman Patrick H. Hodgeson, BPO society president Robert I. Millonzi and B&ECPL Music Department head Ellen Kenney.

open to qualified musicians from anywhere in the world. The player roster began to look like a mini United Nations. The sound this produced was mellow and sophisticated, with a nuance that marked the great orchestras of Europe.

The era was also distinguished by Krips' demand that only the finest soloists share the stage with the BPO. But they did not have to be famous; unknown virtuosity was more than welcome. A fine example of this was when a 20-year-old pianist from Texas was given a chance by Krips to solo with the Buffalo Philharmonic. His name was Van Cliburn, and he first appeared with the BPO on March 13, 1955 in a performance of Schumann's Piano Concerto in A minor. Three years later, Van Cliburn became an international celebrity when he won the first International Tchaikovsky Piano Competition in Moscow.

A 20-YEAR-OLD PIANIST FROM TEXAS WAS GIVEN A CHANCE BY KRIPS TO SOLO... HIS NAME WAS VAN CLIBURN...THREE YEARS LATER, HE WON THE FIRST INTERNATIONAL TCHAIKOVSKY PIANO COMPETITION IN MOSCOW.

With expanding seasons came the need for more scores and parts for the orchestra to perform. Rental costs were prohibitive, so the orchestra began exploring ways to expand its own music library. The first donation to this project came as a $3,000 grant over a period of three years from the Wildroot Foundation of Buffalo, perhaps best remembered for hair cream.

However, when the coveted music library of the National Broadcasting Company Orchestra (NBC) in New York came up for public auction in 1958, Buffalo was quick to react. Funds were collected from generous donors, mostly individual members of the BPO Board of Directors who chose to remain anonymous. The NBC Toscanini Collection of 2,093 titles of orchestral works including scores and parts was purchased by the BPO for $25,000 and donated to the

More than 2,000 nuns from throughout the diocese attend the 1961 annual concert. (*Left to right*) George D'Anna, conductor, Joseph Wincenc, the Rev. Cyril Schommer, S.J., faculty Canisius College, violin.

LP recording of Beethoven

Krips highlights the new sign "Symphony Circle" installed as a temporary name for The Circle, meant to remain only for the duration of the BPO's $150,000 maintenance fund campaign of 1958. The name remains more than 40 years later.

Buffalo & Erie County Public Library. It has served not only the BPO, but also community orchestras throughout Western New York. A charming aspect of this collection is that on many of the scores one can still detect the conductor's artistic markings, from Walter Damrosch (in blue pencil) to Arturo Toscanini (in red pencil). Some of the parts bear the penciled signatures of NBC Orchestra musicians, and many are well thumbed-over.

From the end of the Steinberg era through the tenure of Josef Krips, the Buffalo Philharmonic continued to gain national attention through its many tours – more than 80 tours and run-out concerts in less than a decade. The Orchestra

toured through the Maritime Provinces of Canada in November 1956, but focused on the eastern corridor of New York, Pennsylvania, Massachusetts and Vermont for the remainder of Krips' tenure.

The Orchestra's recording activities consisted of four local LP issues, intended primarily as memoirs for the BPO players and patrons. These included an LP of a WBEN radio broadcast of a live concert on April 4, 1954 of Beethoven's Symphony No.1 under Krips, and also an LP of the live performance of Vaughan Williams' *Sancta Civitas*, conducted by Krips on November 22, 1954. In 1958, a small group of devoted patrons led by Robert Millonzi sponsored a commemorative

continued on page 44

THE BPO TURNS 25

Music Director Josef Krips and pianist Glenn Gould

Just three years after the City of Buffalo celebrated its 125th anniversary, the BPO turned 25.

A Philharmonic Ball kicked off the Orchestra's anniversary on Saturday, November 5, 1960. Sponsored by the Buffalo Philharmonic Women's Committee, the gala evening was held in the Mary Seaton Room and honored Maestro and Mrs. Josef Krips.

The Sunday afternoon Anniversary concert on November 6, 1960 was dedicated to Cameron Baird, Head of the Music Department at the University of Buffalo who had passed away the previous May. Under Krips' baton, the program included *Eagles*, by American composer and UB Slee professor Ned Rorem, Brahms' Symphony No.1, and featured Canadian pianist Glenn Gould in a performance of Beethoven's Piano Concerto No.5 *"Emperor"* that was recorded.* Gould received four curtain calls.

Following the concert, the stage of Kleinhans was quickly converted to host a "linen and silver" reception for performers and audience alike. Board President Franz T. Stone greeted the guests, introduced Mayor Frank Sedita and ceremoniously handed him the baton as a gesture to launch the beginning of a new and festive season.

*This recording was authorized by the American Federation of Musicians for its International Music Fund, and is featured on the *BPO at 75* five-CD Anniversary set.

ZORAH BERRY SERIES

Zorah B. Berry brought hundreds of world class musicians to Buffalo during her 40-year career, many of them appearing in Kleinhans, as well as in the old Elmwood Music Hall and the Consistory before Kleinhans was built.

Buffalo was enjoying its own Golden Age of musical performance when Berry and her husband moved from Detroit to Buffalo in 1922. Following her husband's death shortly after they arrived, she took over the management of the local branch of the Philharmonic Concert Company based in Detroit and within two seasons, assumed ownership.

Building on the concert series begun by Mai Davis Smith and Louis Whiting Gay, Marian de Forest, Michael-Kraft and Bessie Bellanca, the impresario launched Zorah Berry Presents in 1926 with the engagement of world-renowned prima donna Amelita Galli-Curci. The ensuing series in the new Buffalo Consistory Auditorium was successful, both artistically and financially.

The star-studded list of talent brought to Buffalo by Berry is seemingly endless – Ignacy Paderewski, Fritz Kreisler, John

Montevani

Mary Martin

Kirsten Flagstad

Isaac Stern

Enzio Pinza

Yvonne Chouteau

Zorah Berry Presents Concert Series Of

★ HELEN TRA
Soprano
TUESDAY, OCTOBER 12,

HELEN TRAUBEL

★ HEIFETZ
Violinist
TUESDAY, APRIL 19

HEIFETZ

★ BLANC
Mezzo-Soprano
TUESDAY, DEC

BLANCHE THEBOM

★ ISA
Violinist
TUESDAY,

Zorah Berry presents GREATEST ARTIST CONCERT SERIES

"From the scintillating greatness of the familiar names to the blazing brightness of the newer ones—each one of you who listen will tread the pathway to the stars."

eatest All-Star
Year History

★ HOROWITZ ★
Pianist
...BRUARY 8, 1949

HOROWITZ

...LA JONAS ★
Pianist
...OCTOBER 26, 1948

MARYLA JONAS

★ IGOR GORIN ★
Baritone
...SDAY, NOVEMBER 9, 1948

IGOR GORIN

L CANTO TRIO ★
Soprano, Tenor, Bass-Baritone
TUESDAY, JANUARY 11, 1949

L CANTO TRIO

Coming Soon
Zorah Berry
Presents

AT THE MUSIC HALL

J. N. ADAM'S WOMEN'S
DRESSES, FOURTH FLOOR
25.00

Helen
Traubel

Serge
Rachmaninoff

Vladimir
Horowitz

Lily Pons

"Amelita
Galli-Curci"

Paul
Whiteman

McCormack, Sergei Rachmaninoff, Lily Pons, Nelson Eddy, Jeannette MacDonald, Jascha Heifetz, Katharine Cornell...the list is long. The Danish Symphony Orchestra presented a silver medal to Berry as a token of its esteem.

After collaborating with the BPO and complementing the BPO's programming for three decades, the Zorah Berry Concert Series merged with the Buffalo Philharmonic in 1957. The Philharmonic became the sponsor of the Zorah Berry Series for five years, and Berry took charge of the Zorah Berry Division, handling ticket sales for both the BPO and the Zorah Berry Series. Rather than slowing her down, this merger merely allowed Berry to expand the artistic programming to include drama and ballet, as well as mime – Marcel Marceau performed as part of the Series at Kleinhans in 1960.

The Zorah Berry Division was eliminated due to financial constraints at the end of the 1961-62 season, just as maestro Krips departed and before Lukas Foss brought a whole new era to Buffalo. There would be no more regular professional opera in the Queen City.

The seven-volume Zorah B. Berry collection of scrapbooks and photographs spanning 1926-1956, as well as 300 photographs donated by William D. MacPherson, director of the Niagara Lutheran Home where Mrs. Berry died on March 4, 1969, are currently housed in the Grosvenor Room at the Buffalo & Erie County Public Library. They constitute a pictorial and anecdotal history of the concert stage in America.

Commissioned by the New York Power Authority, Ferde Grofe composed and conducted the BPO for the premiere of the *Niagara Falls Suite* at the Niagara University Student Center. The February 4, 1961 performance marked the dedication of the Niagara power project, the largest hydro-electric development in the free world. Robert Moses presented Grofe with a silver baton. The program aired from 10:30-12:00 on Channel 4. That evening, the BPO also performed the same program at a Pops concert in Kleinhans. There was dancing after the concert with Max Miller's Ensemble. It was a long and memorable day.

THE BUFFALO EVENING NEWS, WBEN FEBRUARY 11, 1961

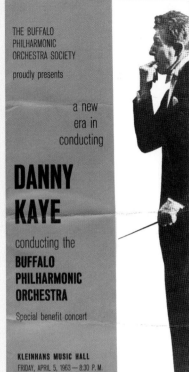

THE BUFFALO PHILHARMONIC ORCHESTRA SOCIETY

proudly presents

a new era in conducting

DANNY KAYE

conducting the

BUFFALO PHILHARMONIC ORCHESTRA

Special benefit concert

KLEINHANS MUSIC HALL
FRIDAY, APRIL 5, 1963 — 8:30 P.M.

A benefit concert, with Danny Kaye and the musicians donating their time and talent.

THE BUFFALO EVENING NEWS, WBEN FEBRUARY 4, 1961

BPO ARCHIVES

John Browning performed the Mozart Piano Concerto No.20 in D Minor, on November 29, 1959.

BPO ARCHIVES

Malcolm Frager performed Prokofief's Concerto No.2 on February 14, 1960.

BPO ARCHIVES

Maestro Krips and composer Vaughan Williams. The BPO performed and recorded Vaughan's *Sancta Civitas* on November 22, 1954.

continued from page 41

local LP issue of Normand Lockwood's *Light Out of Darkness* from performances on February 16 and 18, 1958, also directed by Krips with bass/baritone soloist Yi-Kwei Sze and the Buffalo Schola Cantorum. Another local LP features Grofe's *Niagara Falls Suite*, under the composer's baton, recorded live at the dedication of the Niagara Power Authority on February 10, 1961. The performance of Beethoven's Piano Concerto No.5 *"Emperor,"* featuring soloist Glenn Gould under the baton of Josef Krips, that opened the Orchestra's 25th anniversary season on November 6, 1960, was recorded* with full permissions from the musicians, maestro Krips and Mr. Gould.

The ensemble's first stereo broadcast was an AM/FM simulcast on WBEN, and the orchestra also made its first appearance on television in 1954, when an open rehearsal was aired on WBEN-TV. Telethons for the maintenance fund drive soon became annual events.

A very significant program during this era was the World Frontiers Convocation concert of American Music conducted by Aaron Copland on January 5, 1958 featuring *The Unanswered Question* by Charles Ives. And the Zorah Berry Series merged with the BPO and continued to bring entire productions into Buffalo, including an annual opera.

Pops concerts during the Krips era offered amazingly diverse programs, from "Buffalo Songwriters Night" featuring songs by local lyricist Jack Yellen and conducted by well-known Buffalonian and BPO assistant conductor Joseph Wincenc as part of the 1961 winter Pops series, to "Duke Ellington Night" with the Duke himself and a group of his best-loved tunes and arrangements during the 1961 summer Pops series. Nights of Gershwin, and memorable ballet with Maria Tallchief, among others, thrilled audiences. Maestro Krips himself conducted an annual "Viennese Night," delighting the Pops audience with the melodies of Johann Strauss, Jr.

*Featured on the *BPO at 75* five-CD Anniversary set.

Celebrated violin virtuoso and Buffalo native, Eudice Shapiro soloed six times with the BPO from 1938 through 1982.

WNY songwriter Jack Yellen (*Happy Days are Here Again*), his wife, and Joseph Wincenc.

Buffalo-born Harold Arlen (*Over the Rainbow*), lower right, singing with Judy Garland and the cast of *The Wizard of Oz*.

Salamanca songwriter Ray Evans, known for songs like *Que Será Será*, with his Grammy Award for the song *Dear Heart*.

Cameron Baird had turned his attention from the BPO to the University of Buffalo Music Department, which he founded. Evidence of his presence in both of these musical realms is the two-day Symphony Orchestra Workshop for talented high school juniors and seniors in December 1954, conceived by Baird and BPO manager Ralph Black and co-sponsored by the University of Buffalo and the BPO. Participating students from Buffalo and from as far away as Rochester, NY and Warren, PA participated in more than a dozen workshops and sat side-by-side with members of the Philharmonic to rehearse.

One of the most memorable of many youth and education programs was a children's matinee featuring Broadway's Mary Martin as the airborne Peter Pan.

Financial challenges persisted throughout the Krips years. A "Let There Be Music" billboard urged passersby in February 1957 to "Support Our

LEONARD PENNARIO

Leonard Pennario (1924-2008), born to Sicilian immigrants on Buffalo's Lower West Side, had a dazzling and unusual career.

A prodigy, he was just 12 when he learned the Grieg Concerto in a week and played it, from memory, with the Dallas Symphony Orchestra. He became the best-selling classical pianist of the LP era, recording on Capitol, the cutting-edge label founded by Johnny Mercer.

Because of his popularity and movie-star good looks – he briefly dated Elizabeth Taylor – Pennario was sometimes typecast as a Pops pianist. One person who recognized his real musicianship was the violinist Jascha Heifetz who, in 1961, invited Pennario to join him and the great cellist Gregor Piatigorsky to form a trio.

Pennario, who won a Grammy Award for his work with Heifetz, always maintained his ties to Buffalo, even though he moved to California at the age of 10. Drafted into the U.S. Army Air Corps during World War II, the 18-year-old pianist finagled a brief leave in 1943 so he could make it to Kleinhans Music Hall and play Rachmaninoff's Second Concerto with the Minneapolis Symphony and Dimitri Mitropoulos. He made his debut with the BPO in 1952, playing Tchaikovsky's First Concerto under the baton of William Steinberg.

In the last year of his life – still handsome, and with a wicked sense of humor –

Pennario looked back with special pleasure on concerts he gave with the BPO and Josef Krips. They played Mozart's *"Coronation"* Concerto in 1959, and teamed up again in 1962, when Pennario played the Schumann Concerto for the season-opening gala.

He remembered overhearing Krips and orchestra manager Ramsi Tick bickering amid clouds of cigar smoke over an upcoming Pops concert of hits from *South Pacific*. A wonderful mimic, Pennario put on a thick German accent as he repeated what Krips said: "I do not like the *Enchanted Evening!*"

Because Pennario was famous for large-scale Romantic music, there was one more thing he liked about Krips. "He let me play Mozart."

- MARY KUNZ GOLDMAN

Goldman, music critic for *The Buffalo News*, is working on the authorized biography of Leonard Pennario.

THE BUFFALO EVENING NEWS, FEBRUARY 8, 1957

Business and industry support the BPO fund drive, with a dozen billboards throughout the county. (*Left to right*) President of Whitmier & Ferris Co. John Kress; Women's Committee chair Mrs. John H. Huber, Jr.; co-chairmen of the BPO Board Leroy H. Hurlbert and Kevin Kennedy.

Chamber of Commerce President Jack D. Bunis (*left*) and Buffalo Mayor Frank Sedita (*right*) play trumpet and tuba to the amusement of BPO oboist Rodney Pierce.

THE BUFFALO EVENING NEWS, JUNE 4, 1960

A four-year-old patron purchases her bargain ticket for $1.

COURIER EXPRESS, SEPTEMBER 29, 1958

Mary Martin flies across the Kleinhans stage as Peter Pan with the BPO.

COURIER EXPRESS, DECEMBER 20, 1954

BPO players and students from WNY meet in Kleinhans to take part in a side-by-side symphony workshop and concert directed by Josef Krips.

Orchestra." An emergency drive to raise $1.5 million was launched in June 1960 by Rodney Pierce, head of the orchestra Players Committee. Mayor Frank Sedita and Chamber of Commerce president Jack Bunis both pitched in on the horns to help. Danny Kaye appeared in an "Evening with Danny Kaye," a special benefit performance with the BPO in November 1962. Kaye and the BPO musicians all donated their services to help raise funds to cover a looming $92,000 deficit that threatened to shut the orchestra down in 1963. Although Kaye was known not to read music – making his antics on the podium all the more entertaining – he was actually a brilliant musician, able to memorize a score simply by listening to it a few times. Kaye donated his hysterical services to orchestras across the nation, many of which were in similar financial straits.

Cost-saving measures would eliminate the summer Pops series at the end of the 1961-62 season, a staple since the days of Shuk, as well as the Zorah Berry Division, spelling the end of professional opera – really, the end of an era – in Buffalo.

Although Krips was devoted to Bach and the Classical and Romantic eras, he had an eye for the BPO's future. Just five years after Disneyland became the nation's first theme park, he proposed a two-month summer music festival at Niagara Falls that would include jazz. "Jazz is a true American idiom. But not rock and roll. That is just so much noise." It was hoped that the BPO might find a suitable summer residence, but alas, a full decade would pass before Krips' vision would become Artpark.

A delightful irony finds that Krips' reverence for the classics actually set the stage for the BPO's future as the world's leading orchestra for the avant-garde, and his high European performance standards kept the artistic level high for years to come. The BPO would soon take on a double identity, with one foot in the past, the other in the future.

CHAPTER 6
THE FOSS YEARS

1963-1971

LUKAS FOSS

BORN
August 15, 1922
Berlin, Germany

STUDIED
Piano

DIED
February 1, 2009
New York City, New York

FIRST BPO CONCERT
January 3-5, 1960 (guest conductor)
Bach - *Brandenburg Concerto No.5
in D major*
Bach - *Piano Concerto No.1 in D minor*
Foss - *Chorale Prelude No.2 from
"Symphony of Chorales"*
    Lukas Foss, pianist
Tchaikovsky - *Francesca da
Rimini Fantasia, op.32*

LAST CONCERT AS MUSIC DIRECTOR
April 25-27, 1971
Stravinsky - *Requiem Canticles*
Beethoven - *Symphony No.9 in D minor,
op.125 "Chorale"*
    Nadja Witkowska, soprano
    Joan Caplan, mezzo-soprano
    Allen Cathcart, tenor
    Donald Bell, bass
    Festival Chorus SUNY Fredonia,
        Richard Field, director

RETURN BPO ENGAGEMENTS
December 2 & 3, 1978
January 12 & 13, 1981
February 5 & 6, 1983
December 15 & 16, 1989
September 19 & 20, 1998
April 12 & 13, 2003

BUFFALO HIGHLIGHTS
- BPO Carnegie Hall Debut on
May 1, 1967
- Recordings for Nonesuch of Sibelius,
Cage, Penderecki, Xenakis and Foss
- National PBS TV broadcasts –
Stockhausen's *Momentum* and
Mussorgsky's *Pictures at an Exhibition*
- Premiered his *Renaissance Concerto for
Flute* May 9, 1986
- Established the BPO (and Buffalo) as a
haven and pace-setter for new music
- May 14, 1970 posed with Gov Nelson
Rockefeller and Senator Brydges for the
groundbreaking ceremonies in Lewiston
for Artpark – BPO performed Ravel's
Daphnis and Chloe Suite No.2

CAREER HIGHLIGHTS
- Principal pianist, Boston Symphony
Orchestra, 1944-1951
- Youngest Guggenheim Fellow
in conducting, 1945
- Succeeded Arnold Schoenberg as
professor of composition at UCLA, 1953
- Composed *Echoi* in 1963, widely
regarded as one of the chamber
masterworks of the 20th century
- Music Director, Jerusalem Philharmonic,
Milwaukee Symphony, Brooklyn
Philharmonic

"When we improvise, we work with something we already know. When we compose, we create what we don't know."

- LUKAS FOSS, OCTOBER 6, 1998

Lukas Foss passed away on February 1, 2009 in New York City, at age 86. With poetic irony, the last words spoken by the man who composed Time Cycle were "Wait a moment."

THE FOSS YEARS

1963-1971

BPO MUSICIANS 1963-1964

VIOLIN I
Laszlo Steinhardt, Concertmaster
Harry Taub
Willy Frey
Lawrence Diamond
Ilario Petaro
Zola Cirulli
Miran Viher
Alan Gerstel
Helen Shklar
Genia Palasanian
Clementina Fleshler
Louis Eghian
Charles Petremont
William Hanley
Rivka Mandelkern

VIOLIN II
Igor Prince
Julius Kovach
Laszlo Hajos
Philip Teibel
Charles Coumont

Harry Slick
Oswald Rantucci
Maximilian Huttner
Irene Kutilek
Lois Carson
Meyer Balsom
Darrell Berg

VIOLA
Ascher Temkin
Inti Marshall
Fred Ressel
Edward Gerstel
Elizabeth Phillips
Harold Nissenson
Bernard Fleshler
Mary Hadcock
Felix Frost

CELLO
Dodia Feldin
Yuan Tung
William Brent

William Fahlbusch
Robert Carapetyan
Alfreds Ozolins
Dimitri Carapetyan
Constance Whittaker

STRING BASS
Theodor Mayer
Roger Macchiaroli
Thomas Coleman
William Burns
Frank Primerano
Erling Alfee
Homer Cline

FLUTE
Jacob Berg
Thomas Perazzoli
Laurence Trott

PICCOLO
Laurence Trott

OBOE
Rodney Pierce
Harry VasDias
Florence Myers

ENGLISH HORN
Florence Myers

CLARINET
Peter Hadcock
James Pyne
Edward Yadzinski

E-FLAT CLARINET
James Pyne

BASS CLARINET
Edward Yadzinski

BASSOON
Nelson Dayton
Wilfred Roberts
William Wisler

CONTRABASSOON
William Wisler

FRENCH HORN
Stephen Seiffert
Ginesio Lecce
Lowell Shaw
Barbara Bloomer
Charles McDonald

TRUMPET
Richard Jones
Charles Gleaves
Frank Collura
Eugene Bishop

TROMBONE
Richard Myers
Fred Halt

BASS TROMBONE
Edwin Anderson

TUBA
William Kearney

TIMPANI
George D'Anna

PERCUSSION
John Rowland
Lynn Harbold

HARP
Marjorie Hartzell

PIANO AND CELESTE
Squire Haskin
Rivka Mandelkern

NOTABLE GUEST CONDUCTORS

Aaron Copland, guest conductor | April 21 & 23, 1968

Leonard Bernstein, composer, conductor | March 14 & 15, 1964

Luciano Berio, composer, conductor | December 12 & 14, 1965

Ingolf Dahl, composer, conductor | March 1, 1965

Sergiu Comissiona, guest conductor | March 14 & 16, 1971

Eleazar de Carvalho, conductor | January 15 & 17, 1967

Walter Hendl, conductor | May 6, 1967

John Cage, composer, conductor | May 28, 1967

Walter Susskind, conductor | January 12 & 14, 1969

Michael Tilson Thomas, guest conductor | November 22 & 24, 1970

Julius Rudel, guest conductor | February 7 & 9, 1971

Sixten Ehrling, guest conductor | March 23 & 25, 1969

NOTABLE GUEST SOLOISTS

André Watts, pianist | November 24 & 26, 1963

Isaac Stern, violinist | December 15 & 17, 1963

Leonard Rose, cellist | January 12 & 14, 1964

Alexander Brailowsky, pianist | November 15 & 17, 1964

Itzhak Perlman, violinist | December 6 & 8, 1964

Adele Addison, soprano | January 10 & 12, 1965

Ruggiero Ricci, violinist | January 17 & 19, 1965

Janos Starker, cellist | February 7 & 9, 1965

Rudolf Serkin, pianist | March 21 & 23, 1965

Senator Jacob K. Javitts, narrator | February 20 & 22, 1966

Andres Segovia, guitarist | April 3 & 5, 1966

Leonard Pennario, pianist | March 20 & 22, 1966

Marni Nixon, soprano | October 30 & November 1, 1966

Zino Francescatti, violinist | February 19 & 21, 1967

Claudio Arrau, pianist | February 26 & 28, 1967

Mstislav Rostropovich, cellist | May 28, 1967

Bethany Beardslee, soprano | May 28, 1967

Eileen Farrell, soprano | October 21 & 24, 1967

Nathan Milstein, violinist | January 21 & 23, 1968

Witold Malcuzynski, pianist | February 4 & 6, 1968

Yuji Takahshi, pianist | March 10 & 12, 1968

Van Cliburn, pianist | March 24 & 26, 1968

Roberta Peters, soprano | October 19 & 22, 1968

Robert Casadesus, pianist | October 27 & 29, 1968

Vladimir Ashkenazy, pianist | November 17 & 19, 1968

Erica Morini, violinist | January 19 & 21, 1969

Cifford Curzon, pianist | February 9 & 11, 1969

Leonid Kogan, violinist | February 16 & 18, 1969

Mstislav Rostropovich, cellist | March 16 & 18, 1969

Henryk Szeryng, violinist | April 20 & 22, 1969

Charles Haupt, violinist | October 26 & 28, 1969

Christopher Parkening, guitar | November 9 & 11, 1969

Ivry Gitlis, violinist | November 16 & 18, 1969

Phyllis Curtin, soprano | December 7 & 9, 1969

Yehudi Menuhin, violinist | January 25 & 27, 1970

Maureen Forrester, contralto | May 10 & 12, 1970

Igor Oistrakh, violinist | January 24 & 26, 1971

CHAIRMEN OF THE BPO BOARD OF DIRECTORS

1962-1963 Mr. David J. Laub

1964-1965 Mr. Clarence Obletz

1966-1967 Mr. A. John MacDonald

1968-1969 Mr. George F. Goodyear

1970-1973 Mr. Peter P. Poth

THE FOSS YEARS

1963-1971

While every decade brings change, it is unlikely that any surpasses that ushered in during the 1960s. The escalating war in Vietnam, the burgeoning civil rights movement, the women's and gay liberation movements – all were manifestations of a deep discontent, a generational divide and a desire for new, modern, different.

If ever the arts mirrored history in almost perfect alignment, it was during this tumultuous period. John Cage composed his controversial *4'33"* featuring a pianist on stage sitting in silence – the only way the listener knew if the piece progressed to the next movement was by the raising or lowering of the piano lid; Merce Cunningham choreographed dances with broad, bold movements which embodied a grace all their own; Jackson Pollock was first to take his canvas off the wall, put it on the floor, then drip, even throw the paint, creating art that was wild, exciting and new. Longtime Buffalo professor and resident Robert Creeley wrote, "when a man makes a poem, makes it mind you, he takes the words as he finds them lying interrelated about him."

The arts were awakening emotions in the human spirit that screamed, stomped and squeezed audiences all over the world like never before. But what made these times so poignant for the BPO was that the whole world seemed to be watching Buffalo, New York.

BPO ARCHIVES

Lukas Foss during a recording session.

Three critical events in 1962 helped thrust Buffalo into the unexpected position of avant-garde bellwether.

First, Seymour H. Knox donated a new wing to the Albright Art Gallery to house his extraordinary collection of what was coming to be known as "modern art." The dynamic new Albright-Knox Art Gallery energized the arts community and brought international attention to Buffalo. The sleek, new auditorium married music and art, providing the perfect venue for hundreds of innovative musical programs over the coming decades.

Then the State University of New York completed its takeover of the venerable University of Buffalo, creating the State University of New York at Buffalo, or SUNYAB, igniting a period of unprecedented expansion and excitement. The intention was to create an intellectual and cultural mecca. It succeeded, attracting an amazing array of talented artists, writers and musicians who quickly formed an intellectual and creative community that thrived in Buffalo's close-knit environment.

WHEN THE BUFFALO PHILHARMONIC WAS THE BOSTON POPS

Program for the BPO masquerading as the Boston Pops under Arthur Fiedler in the spring of 1964.

Conductor Melvin Strauss, violinist Julius Kovach and Zola Cirulli check a score in 1967.

One for the Fiddle...Two for the Bow...

A cartoon of the BPO principle trio featured in the *Courier Express* in March 1971. Violinist Charles Haupt, violist Jesse Levine and cellist Wolfram Reuthe appear as soloists.

The BPO playing in the Erie County Home in 1970, conducted by John Landis.

The Buffalo Philharmonic has toured under guest maestros as diverse as Aaron Copland and Walter Hendl, always as the Buffalo Philharmonic Orchestra. But when the legendary Arthur Fiedler conducted the BPO on a long tour of the eastern half of the U.S. in 1964, they toured as the Boston Pops. Nearly every one of the 24 cities on the tour was a sell-out, and concert venues included Chicago; Manchester, NH; and Washington, DC.

In 1964-65, Fiedler once again asked the Buffalo Philharmonic to tour with him, but the musicians insisted that the concerts be billed as "Arthur Fiedler and the Buffalo Pops Orchestra." Fiedler agreed with a smile, as he knew the concerts would be sold-out – and they were! The 21 concert venues included Austin, TX; Lincoln, NB; and Lake Charles, LA.

For its part, the BPO named Lukas Foss as its new music director. Robert Millonzi had been impressed with Foss when he guest conducted a BPO program in 1960 that included a movement from Foss' own composition, *Symphony of Chorales*. Allen Sapp, who succeeded Cameron Baird as chairman of UB's meteoric Music Department and sat on the BPO Board of Directors, also strongly supported hiring the articulate, young music director. Foss, UCLA Schoenberg professor of composition and conducting, assumed the helm as the new music director of the Buffalo Philharmonic, setting firmly in place the third leg of the proverbial stool that set Buffalo on its ear.

Opening night concertgoers were at once enchanted by Ives' *Unanswered Question*, then thrilled by the flash and peal of Stravinsky's *Rite of Spring*. Foss and his initial program exuded a youthful, Kennedy-esque energy, and he was considered an immediate success.

A telling hallmark of the Foss years was the decision to premiere in Buffalo several new pieces each season, often including national and world premieres. It kept everyone guessing. He managed to premiere unusual, lesser-known pieces, or simply works that had not been performed in Buffalo like Strauss' *Ein Heldenleben*. At one point, the Buffalo Philharmonic had presented more American premieres in a one-year period than all

THE BUFFALO EVENING NEWS, FEBRUARY 14, 1970

Pop soloist Duke Ellington performs a Valentine's Day Concert in 1970.

BPO ARCHIVES

Violinist Pinkas Zuckerman performed Lalo's Symphonie Espagnole on November 8, 1970.

THE BUFFALO EVENING NEWS, APRIL 15, 1966

COURIER EXPRESS, MARCH 14, 1971

Pablo Casals conducts a BPO rehearsal in April 1966.

Pianist Eugene Istomin performs Schumann's Piano Concerto in March 1971.

BPO ARCHIVES

other major U.S. orchestras combined. *This Sacred Ground*, written by David Diamond on commission for *The Buffalo Evening News* to celebrate the centennial of "Gettysburg Address," premiered on November 17, 1963, was broadcast worldwide on CBS, and was reviewed in the *New York Times* and on UPI. In March 1964, Dr. Karlheinz Stockhausen conducted the BPO in the North American premiere of his *Momente*. It was covered exclusively by the New York press, videotaped by National Educational TV (later PBS) and broadcast nationwide in a pair of hour-long programs. And this was just the beginning of the intense media focus on Buffalo.

THE PREMIERE OF *THIS SACRED GROUND* CELEBRATING THE CENTENNIAL OF THE GETTYSBURG ADDRESS IS BROADCAST WORLDWIDE ON CBS.

Locally, *The Buffalo Evening News*, long a staunch supporter of the orchestra, continued to play an important role. Music critic John Dwyer understood the importance of what was happening in Kleinhans and carefully crafted his words to encourage the public to listen with new ears. WBEN-TV pitched in by airing an 11-program series during Foss' first season about the new and different music to be heard in Kleinhans.

The BPO musicians stepped up to the challenge of performing new music, as well. Foss did a masterful job of enlisting their support, assisted by associate conductor Richard Dufallo and principal violist

Aaron Copland once described Foss' music as "among the most original and stimulating compositions in American music." After a particularly complex avant-garde concert by the BPO in the late 1960s, Foss was asked, "After all these incredible sounds, what will new music sound like 200 years from now?" Foss replied: "Eh...There is no way to know. But if I knew, I would compose it right now!"

Leonard Bernstein and Lukas Foss
on stage in Kleinhans during a rehearsal in 1964.

During the 1960s, bridging old and new music became a primary challenge for orchestras and conductors throughout the world. One of the primary musical figures of the era was Leonard Bernstein, who was already renowned for developing new listeners through his Young People's Concerts with the New York Philharmonic. On March 14, 1964, as a last minute substitution for André Previn, he flew to Buffalo to perform an all-Bernstein program with Lukas Foss and the BPO. Bernstein conducted the *Age of Anxiety* Symphony No.2, with Foss as piano soloist. Foss conducted *Candide* Overture and *Symphonic Dances* from *West Side Story*. Upon being asked by *The Buffalo News* about all the new music being programmed by Foss in Buffalo, Bernstein replied: "More power to him. No art is old. Any art that is contemporary, that is alive, must involve what is going on now."

Foss directed the first Buffalo Festival of the Arts Today in February 1968. The event drew more than 180,000 attendees and significant international attention, including this article in the *Toronto Daily Star*.

Jesse Levine, both of whom stood firmly behind him. There were times when it was more challenging than others. However there was never any doubt about the incredible musicianship of the music director, and it helped when the orchestra was featured on national television broadcasts and received national and international press attention. Foss came to be known as "The Man Who Turned Buffalo On."

Onto this exciting scene there arrived the perfect way to fuse the energy in Kleinhans with the

Several of the creative associates with the UB Center of the Creative and Performing Arts at rehearsal.

growing excitement on campus. In March 1964, a Rockefeller Foundation start-up grant launched the Center of the Creative and Performing Arts, a professional chamber ensemble at SUNY Buffalo. SUNYAB Music Department chairman Allen Sapp and Lukas Foss were named co-directors and went to work scouring the globe for 18 to 20 composer-performer virtuosi with a passion for new music. The Center was unique, marking the first time a university had provided full time support for an ensemble of this size dedicated solely to

BPO ARCHIVES

North American New Music Festival 1990 Program

BPO ARCHIVES

North American New Music Festival 1992 Poster

BPO ARCHIVES

North American New Music Festival 10th Anniversary brochure

performing, not teaching. The Center is affectionately described by Renee Levine-Packer in her book *This Life of Sounds* as "an artist's colony within a university." But the musicians lived in Buffalo, many on the West Side, and quickly found themselves collaborating with BPO musicians in both formal and informal ways. A full season of concerts was offered at the Albright-Knox Art Gallery Auditorium under the baton of Foss.

Another valuable collaboration resulted in the Buffalo Festival of the Arts Today, cosponsored by the BPO and the Albright-Knox Art Gallery. Alongside the innovative art, dance, theater and poetry were two memorable concerts by the BPO during the first Festival in March 1965, featuring works by Cage, Feldman, Kagel, Penderecki and others. *LIFE* magazine did a several page spread on the innovative Festival and Buffalo, branding the Queen City as the epicenter of new music. This attracted young composers and musicians to Buffalo from across the nation.

Then the State Department invited the BPO to participate in the Organization of America States (OAS) Inter-American Music Festival, drawing international attention to Buffalo. The American Society of Composers, Authors and Publishers (ASCAP) honored Foss' programming and the Orchestra also received a $1.75 million Ford Foundation matching grant. The BPO had emerged from its conservative cocoon as one of the most radical orchestras in the world and newspapers and magazines around the globe began touting Buffalo as a modern mecca for the arts.

In October 1966 the BPO performed the world premiere of two newly discovered orchestral songs by Anton Webern with repeat performances at Carnegie Hall and the Place des Arts in Montreal, Canada.

Despite all the excitement surrounding new music and the BPO's growing reputation and the consequent demands placed on it, the orchestra still managed to go on a number of tours.

continued on page 57

CARNEGIE HALL

The Buffalo Philharmonic performed the first of the Orchestra's more than 20 concerts at Carnegie Hall on May 1, 1967, under the baton of Lukas Foss, featuring pianist Charles Rosen. Bach's Concerto in C Minor for Oboe and Violin was followed by two Webern works, Pärt's *Perpetuo Mobile*, and Ravel's Piano Concerto in G Major and Daphnis and Chloé Suite No.2.

Coincidentally, this debut performance by the BPO opened Carnegie Hall's 75th Diamond Jubilee season, a wonderful connection to the BPO's own 75th Anniversary celebration in 2010.

The BPO returned to Carnegie Hall three more times under Foss, in September 1968, May 1969 and March 1970.

Michael Tilson Thomas would take the Orchestra to Carnegie Hall no fewer than a dozen times between 1973 and 1979.

Julius Rudel conducted the BPO in Carnegie Hall in November 1980, but more than five years would pass before the Orchestra returned with Semyon Bychkov in February 1986. Two additional appearances in February and October 1988 under Bychkov completes this cycle. A full 15 years passed until the next two performances in Carnegie Hall in June 2004 under the baton of JoAnn Falletta.

Carnegie Hall program covers

CD cover of the BPO performance at Carnegie Hall recorded on June 6, 2004

COURIER EXPRESS, 1970

Movie Night at the BPO Pops, from *Mary Poppins* to *Zorba the Greek.*

THE BUFFALO EVENING NEWS, DECEMBER 26, 1970

Members of the Buffalo band The Raven meet with Lukas Foss before appearing with the orchestra in 1970. Seated with Foss is Jim Calire; standing (*from left to right*) are Tony Galla, Tom Calandra, Gary Mallabar and John Weitz.

BPO ARCHIVES

Live Session program books. The New Music tradition at UB continued into the Bychkov years.

After performing as the Boston Pops on tour under Arthur Fiedler in 1964, the BPO quickly resumed its own name and was on-the-road for as many as nine weeks in a single season, resulting in the grand sum of 124 tour concerts during the Foss years, covering New England and the southern states, as well as the Midwest, from Nebraska to Texas.

"American Music in the Universities" was a tour designed to bring contemporary American music to college campuses throughout New York State in May 1967. The performance on May 29 featured the master of outrage, John Cage, at the podium conducting his *Concerto for Prepared Piano* with Lukas Foss at the piano, the world premiere of Foss' Cello Concerto performed by Mstislav Rostropovich, and Robert Marvel's Canzona Symphonic.

In April 1968, Aaron Copland guest conducted the BPO in Lockport, NY; Bradford, PA; Danbury, CN; and Rutland, VT. He also performed as soloist with members of the BPO in a Chamber Music concert on Saturday afternoons at the Buffalo & Erie County Public Library.

The highpoints of the BPO's extensive tours in the late 1960s were undoubtedly the Orchestra's debut appearances in Lincoln Center on December 21, 1964 and in Carnegie Hall on May 1, 1967, followed by a performance at Montreal's Expo '67, all under Foss. The orchestra would return to Lincoln Center with Foss in December 1967, and would return many times to Carnegie Hall over the following decades.

The Orchestra's Pops programs featured The Music of Hollywood, A Night in Vienna, Ballet Night and The Music of Broadway, but it was the era of classical

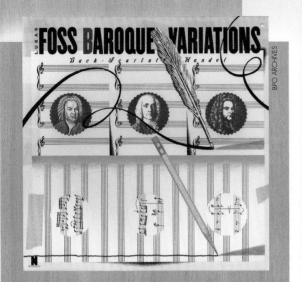

Pickwick Puppet Theater presents Tchaikovsky's *Sleeping Beauty* with the BPO, a Family Concert on April 3, 1971.

Dave Thomas and Promo the Robot on WKBW-TV perform *Babar the Little Elephant* with the BPO on April 13, 1971.

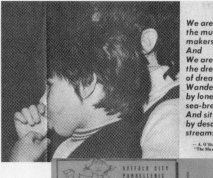

We are
the music-
makers,
And
We are
the dreamers
of dreams,
Wandering
by lone
sea-breakers,
And sitting
by desolate
streams.

— A. O'Shaughnessy in
"The Music-Makers"

BUFFALO CITY
PANHELLENIC
presents
THE BUFFALO PHILHARMONIC ORCHESTRA

KINDER KONZERT

TUESDAY, MARCH 31, 1970 – 2 O'CLOCK
KLEINHANS MUSIC HALL

Captivated child attending a Kinder Konzert in 1972.

Foss said of *Baroque Variations*, one of his three new recordings on the Nonesuch label: "...they are dreams about the music of the Baroque composers... about the inaudible music in the Handel variation. I composed the holes."

- LUKAS FOSS
September 1968

---

jazz and rock & roll. The BPO performed in concert with Duke Ellington and even invited the local band The Raven on stage. The most memorable rock concert, however, is surely with the Grateful Dead, in a spectacular four-hour concert marathon on March 17, 1970 with Lukas Foss on the podium. After an opening jam session, the BPO and the Grateful Dead alternated sets, joining for Foss' *Geod*. A brief experimental work called *Challenge* was improvised on the spot by Foss, in which the rock group and the BPO were featured together in a battle of the bands. Outrageous.

AFTER AN OPENING JAM SESSION, THE BPO AND THE GRATEFUL DEAD ALTERNATED SETS. *CHALLENGE* WAS IMPROVISED ON THE SPOT BY FOSS. OUTRAGEOUS!

The BPO's educational outreach offered an average of 60 youth concerts each season, most in Kleinhans Music Hall. The "FM School of the Air" in 1964, however, broadcast a series of youth concerts that were aired in schools throughout New York State. Among the special offerings for youngsters in Kleinhans during these heady years were Kinder Konzerts, with delightful programs like Poulenc's *Babar the Elephant* and Britten's *Young Person's Guide to the Orchestra*. Dave Thomas and Promo the Robot of "Rocketship 7" fame appeared with the BPO, with Promo playing the piano and conducting. The Pickwick Puppet Theater presented Tchaikovsky's

NORTH AMERICAN NEW MUSIC FESTIVAL
DEPARTMENT OF MUSIC
APRIL 21-30 1987
STATE UNIVERSITY OF NEW YORK AT BUFFALO
BPO ARCHIVES

NANMF 1988
BPO ARCHIVES

NORTH AMERICAN NEW MUSIC FESTIVAL
DEPARTMENT OF MUSIC
STATE UNIVERSITY OF NEW YORK AT BUFFALO
MARCH 10-19 1988
BPO ARCHIVES

NORTH AMERICAN NEW MUSIC FESTIVAL
DEPARTMENT OF MUSIC
APRIL 10-20 1986
STATE UNIVERSITY OF NEW YORK AT BUFFALO
BPO ARCHIVES

Sleeping Beauty, with four- and five-foot puppets performing to music by the BPO under the baton of Melvin Strauss.

March 1968 would prove to be the apex of the Foss era.

The Second Annual Festival of the Arts at UB took place as scheduled in March 1968, directed by Foss and Allen Sapp. The second festival was even more spectacular than the first. It was covered by both *TIME* and *High Fidelity* magazines, and *Baroque Variations* was televised by the Public Broadcast Laboratory (now PBS). For this, the BPO was awarded "distinguished performance of American music written since 1940." The BPO performed in Kleinhans Music Hall, the Creative Associates at UB, Merce Cunningham Dance Company at Buffalo State College and Evenings for New Music at the Albright-Knox Art Gallery.

Also in March 1968, Foss and the BPO broke major ground by recording three LPs for the Nonesuch label, two of which featured new scores from the

DAVE THOMAS AND PROMO THE ROBOT OF *ROCKETSHIP 7* FAME APPEARED WITH THE BPO. PROMO PLAYED THE PIANO AND "CONDUCTED" THE ORCHESTRA.

avant-garde, including the music of Xenakis, Penderecki, Cage and the first complete recording of Foss' exquisite *Baroque Variations*. The third LP was devoted to Sibelius' *Four Legends from Kalevala*. Foss later recorded his experimental *Geod* on the Vox/Candide label as well as the music of Copland, Ives, Ruggles and Subotnick for Turnabout/Vox.

It is difficult to understand why an era of such wonderful creativity would be plagued by financial uncertainty, but it was, despite funding by the new National Endowment for the Arts and Humanities and increasing government support. On April 4, 1968 it was unexpectedly announced that the orchestra could potentially close its doors if the Maintenance Fund Drive were to fall short. A benefit concert introduced by Jack Benny was broadcast by all four local television stations, and D'Youville College premiered *2001: A Space Odyssey* to raise funds for the Philharmonic. Shortfalls would continue.

PEANUTS

Music means so much more when you're there.

Order Season Tickets Buffalo Philharmonic Orchestra 885-5000

An unusual contribution to the BPO effort to attract audiences of all ages to Kleinhans and to support the Orchestra's Maintenance Fund came in the form of a Peanuts poster. In January 1967 Hans Vigeland, choirmaster at Westminster Presbyterian Church and Buffalo Seminary teacher, wrote to his favorite pen pal, Schroeder. Their correspondence began in 1962 when Vigeland sent a card to Schroeder from Beethoven's birthplace. Legendary cartoonist Charles Schulz generously donated to the BPO a custom-drawn cartoon of pianist Schroeder and Snoopy with the caption "Music means so much more when you're there."

"Save the Philharmonic" Campaign spokesman and BPO oboist, Rodney Pierce (*right*) presents musicians' check to the BPO Society as their part of the Annual Fund Drive in 1970.

BPO musicians' "Save the Philharmonic Campaign" woodwind quintet performs in Main Place Mall. (*From left to right*) Spokesperson Clementina Fleshler, picciloist Lawrence Trott, oboist Rodney Pierce, french hornist Lowell Shaw, clarinetist Russ Dagon, bassoonist Ron Daniels.

In 1969, when the BPO Society proposed a merger between the Buffalo Philharmonic and the Rochester Philharmonic, the Buffalo musicians responded with a "Save the Philharmonic" campaign, playing trios and quintets at local malls and on street corners, even offering continuous chamber music at the Allentown Arts Festival. Although the players raised only $40,000, they succeeded in generating so much public support and attention that city, county and state funding was finally forthcoming. The rescue monies came with strings attached, however: more populist programming. The great merger crisis had been averted, but not without the loss of Foss, who announced that he would resign when his contract ended in 1971. Little known is the fact that he recommended Michael Tilson Thomas to succeed him on the podium in Kleinhans. Foss liked to say, "The past is prologue."

These were heady times indeed, Buffalo's own Age of Enlightenment. In a special way, those days will truly never end, as Buffalo's creative energy still echoes around the world in major arts venues.

CHAPTER 7

THE TILSON THOMAS YEARS

1971-1979

MICHAEL TILSON THOMAS

BORN
December 21, 1944
Los Angeles, California

STUDIED
Piano

CURRENTLY
Music Director of the San Francisco
Symphony

FIRST BPO CONCERT
November 22, 1970 (guest conductor)
Mozart - *Violin Concerto No.4
in D major, K.218*
    Kyung Wha Chung, violinist
Mahler - *Symphony No.5 in C-sharp minor*

LAST CONCERT AS MUSIC DIRECTOR
May 15, 1979
Mahler - *Symphony No.3 in D minor*
    Florence Quivar, mezzo-soprano
    Women's Chorus of the Buffalo
    Schola Cantorum,
        Peter Perret, director
    St. Paul's Boy's Choir,
        Anthony Furnivall, director

RETURN BPO ENGAGEMENTS
October 21 & 23, 1979
November 11 & 13, 1979
December 6 & 9, 1980
February 20 & 22, 1981
January 8 & 9, 1983
December 4 & 5, 1987
March 17, 2001

BPO ARCHIVES

BUFFALO HIGHLIGHTS
- Tours to New York, Boston, Chicago, Washington DC, Florida
- Recordings for Columbia, including Gershwin overtures, borrowed by Woody Allen, for his film *Manhattan*
- Conducted the BPO dedication of Artpark in 1974

CAREER HIGHLIGHTS
- Music Director (at age 19) of the Young Musicians' Foundation Debut Orchestra
- Worked on premieres with Stravinsky, Copland and Stockhausen
- Won the Koussevitzky Prize at Tanglewood in 1969
- Named music director of the San Francisco Symphony in 1995.
- Principal Guest Conductor, Los Angeles Philharmonic, 1981-1985
- Received the National Medal of Arts, the nation's highest award for artistic achievement, presented by President Barack Obama on February 25, 2010 at the White House

"I raise my hands: invite them to meet me in psycho-acoustic space: we find the music together...miraculous!"

- MICHAEL TILSON THOMAS

THE TILSON THOMAS YEARS

1971-1979

BPO MUSICIANS 1971-1972

VIOLIN I
Charles Haupt, Concertmaster
Harry Taub
Zola Cirulli
Igor Prince
Marie Yadzinski
Donald McCrorey
Matthew Tworek
Ernst Auerbah
Frances Bagdol
Marylouise Nanna
Clementina Fleshler
Nancy Meinhard
Karen Farrar
Dennis Piwowarski
Chan Young Kim
Rivka Mandelkern
John Mikulin

VIOLIN II
Marilynn Kregal
Julius Kovach
Laszlo Hajos

Philip Teibel
Charles Coumont
Harry Slick
Oswald Rantucci
Maximilian Huttner
Irena Coumont
Diane Melillo
Stanley King
Kurt Brychta
Lois Carson
Meyer Balsom

VIOLA
Jesse Levine
Edward Gerstel
Inti Marshall
Frank Reilly
Elizabeth Phillips
Harold Nissenson
Bernard Fleshler
Shuntatsu Kohno
Fred Ressel

CELLO
Wolfram Reuthe
Robert Carapetyan
Dodia Feldin
Mary Lane
Monte Hoffman
Alta Mayer
Dimitri Carapetyan
Mary Sue Wells
Alden Ring
Constance Miller

STRING BASS
Theodor Mayer
Roger Macchiaroli
William Burns
Frank Primerano
John Haas
Makoto Michii
Nicholas Molfese
Louis Bruno

FLUTE
John Burgess
Eiko Ito
Laurence Trott

PICCOLO
Laurence Trott

OBOE
Rodney Pierce
Colin Smith
Florence Myers

ENGLISH HORN
Florence Myers

CLARINET
James Pyne
Daniel Johnston
Edward Yadzinski

E-FLAT CLARINET
Daniel Johnston

BASS CLARINET AND SAXOPHONE
Edward Yadzinski

BASSOON
Nelson Dayton
David Beadle
Ronald Daniels

CONTRABASSOON
Ronald Daniels

FRENCH HORN
William Lane
Roy Waas
Lowell Shaw
Fred Bradford
Milton Kicklighter

TRUMPET
David Kuehn
Charles Gleaves
Gerald Soffer
Frank Collura

TROMBONE
Richard Myers
Fred Halt

BASS TROMBONE
Donald Miller

TUBA
Ellis Wean

TIMPANI
Jesse Kregal

PERCUSSION
Lynn Harbold
John Rowland

HARP
Suzanne Thomas

KEYBOARDS
Rivka Mandelkern
Clementina Fleshler

NOTABLE GUEST CONDUCTORS

Julius Rudel, guest conductor | January 9 & 11, 1972

Werner Torkanowsky, guest conductor | January 23 & 25, 1972

Sergiu Comissiona, guest conductor | January 7 & 9, 1973

Edo de Waart, guest conductor | January 19 & 20, 1974

Maurice Abravanel, guest conductor | March 30 & 31, 1974

Neville Marriner, guest conductor | October 19 & 20, 1974

Leonard Slatkin, conductor | March 9 & 11, 1975

Jorge Mester, guest conductor | February 15 & 17, 1976

Sarah Caldwell, guest conductor | October 29 & 30, 1977

John Mauceri, guest conductor | January 20 & 21, 1979

NOTABLE GUEST SOLOISTS

Alex Weissenberg, pianist | March 11 & 13, 1973

Alicia de Larrocha, pianist | October 7 & 8, 1978

André Watts, pianist | November 18 & 20, 1973

Anthony Newman, harpsichordist | February 4 & 6, 1973

Cathy Berberian, soprano | April 21 & 23, 1974

Christoph Eschenbach, pianist | February 19 & 22, 1972

Clamma Dale, soprano | February 11 & 12, 1978

Eileen Farrel, soprano | January 25 & 27, 1976

Emanuel Ax, pianist | December 3 & 4, 1977

Erik Friedman, violinist | January 19 & 20, 1974

Eugene Istomin, pianist | January 18 & 20, 1976

Frederica von Stade, soprano | February 10 & 12, 1974

Garrick Ohlsson, pianist | October 16 & 19, 1971

Gary Graffman, pianist | March 21 & 23, 1976

Henryk Szeryng, violinist | November 11 & 13, 1973

Horacio Gutierrez, pianist | March 12 & 13, 1978

Ilana Vered, pianist | January 7 & 9, 1973

Isaac Stern, violinist | April 23 & 25, 1972

Itzhak Perlman, violinist | April 9 & 11, 1972

James Buswell, violinist | February 8 & 9, 1975

Jessye Norman, soprano | October 27 & 29, 1974

John Browning, pianist | March 23 & 25, 1975

Kyung Wha Chung, violinist | November 2 & 3, 1974

Leonard Pennario, pianist | February 27 & 29, 1972

Leonard Rose, cellist | March 9 & 11, 1975

Lorin Hollander, pianist | October 23 & 25, 1977

Malcolm Frager, pianist | April 28 & 30, 1974

Misha Dichter, pianist | April 8 & 10, 1973

Pinchas Zukerman, violinist | April 22 & 24, 1979

Ruggiero Ricci, violinist | March 30 & 31, 1974

Ruth Laredo, pianist | April 9 & 11, 1978

Charles Haupt, violinist | May 9 & 11, 1976

Ursula Oppens, pianist | November 7 & 9, 1976

Vladimir Ashkenazy, pianist | February 25 & 27, 1973

Walter Cronkite, narrator | May 14, 1977

Zara Nelsova, cellist | February 22 & 24, 1976

CHAIRMEN OF THE BPO BOARD OF DIRECTORS

1970-1973 Mr. Peter P. Poth

1974 Mr. C. Victor Raiser II

1975-1976 Mr. Edwin Polokoff

1977-1978 Mr. James H. Righter

1978acting Mr. John N. Walsh III

1979 Mr. G. Wayne Hawk

THE TILSON THOMAS YEARS

1971-1979

This era of opposing viewpoints created the best and worst of times. The war in Vietnam ended in 1975, but not before protests rocked the nation. Like many campuses across the country, the University at Buffalo saw tear gas canisters and marches interrupt classes and exams. There was a culture of distrust. Growing concerns about the environment sparked the first Earth Day in April 1970, and the Blizzard of '77 would blanket Buffalo, silencing all activity for a week. A driving ban was in effect and Kleinhans Music Hall remained dark.

Michael Tilson Thomas first came to the BPO as a guest conductor in November 1970. However, it was his brilliant emergency substitution for William Steinberg halfway through an October 1969 concert in New York City that first brought the Boston Symphony assistant conductor to the attention of the BPO – and indeed, the entire orchestra world. Tilson Thomas apparently also had his eye on Buffalo, and had been contemplating becoming a Creative Associate with SUNY Buffalo's Center of the Creative and Performing Arts. Instead, on February 19, 1971, Tilson Thomas became one of the youngest music directors ever appointed.

Just 27 years old, Tilson Thomas brought youth and verve – and even more media attention – to the BPO. *The New York Times Magazine* ran a cover story on the *wunderkind* in October 1971 that compared him to the young Leonard Bernstein. Despite their economic woes, Buffalo and the BPO remained up front and center in the philharmonic realm.

NEW YORK TIMES MAGAZINE, 1971

Michael Tilson Thomas is featured in the *New York Times Magazine* following his BPO appointment in 1971.

The young conductor's Opening program started with Haydn's *Farewell Symphony*, followed by Liszt and Beethoven. Perhaps out to prove his mettle and with a nod to the Bernstein comparisons, during his very first season, Tilson Thomas conquered *Turangalîla-Symphonie*, the large-scale piece by Olivier Messiaen commissioned by the Boston Symphony Orchestra, which Leonard Bernstein unexpectedly premiered in 1949, substituting for Serge Koussevitzky who had fallen ill. Tilson Thomas clearly intended to maintain the adventurous programming of Foss, and made a point of programming new music, but soon put his own stamp on the creative persona of the BPO.

The BPO made it through the fiscal crisis of 1969-70. A new General Manager position was filled by businessman Howard Bradley, who also was named President of the Board of Directors, which was pared down and put under

COURIER EXPRESS, SEPTEMBER 28, 1975

Michael Tilson Thomas working to create an advertisement on a computer (in the background) for the 1975-76 season, aided by UB composer Lejaren Hiller.

BPO ARCHIVES

BPO Musicians portrait. (*From left to right*) Roy Waas, Nicholas Molfese, Frances Kaye, Suzanne Thomas, Robert Carapetyan and Richard Kay.

BPO ARCHIVES

Michael Tilson Thomas at rehearsal in Kleinhans.

BPO ARCHIVES

GEORGE GERSHWIN
RHAPSODY IN BLUE
GEORGE GERSHWIN, Piano
(The 1925 Piano Roll)
AN AMERICAN IN PARIS
BROADWAY OVERTURES
MICHAEL TILSON THOMAS, Dir.

BPO recording of *Broadway Overtures* by George Gershwin under the baton of Michael Tilson Thomas.

the purview of a new Board of Trustees. An aggressive fund drive was launched and new marketing strategies were developed. Over the next few years, QRS Music Rolls on Niagara Street promoted a concert series of solo artists in Kleinhans Music Hall and Shea's Buffalo Theater was restored, marking the beginning of the revitalization of the theater district in downtown Buffalo.

There were many instances when Tilson Thomas spun a new idea into gold. One of them was planning the 1975-76 season in keeping with the nation's bicentennial celebration and commissioning Lejaren Hiller, local composer and head of the Center of the Creative and Performing Arts, to create an advertisement for the BPO season on the computer. This was a brand new concept in 1975.

THE BUFFALO EVENING NEWS, 1974

BPO violinist Marylouise Nanna in her role as music director of the Ars Nova Chamber Orchestra.

Another project was visiting QRS Music Rolls in 1977 and obtaining a George Gershwin piano roll of *Rhapsody in Blue* with Gershwin at the keyboard. Tilson Thomas recorded the piece with an *ad hoc* orchestra as though the composer were there himself. The recording also features six Gershwin Overtures by the BPO.

The big news in the 1973-74 season was the opening of Artpark. It took the efforts of three consecutive BPO music directors to bring this dream to fruition. Conceived by Krips as a summer home for the BPO, it was supported through the long political process by Foss, and finally inaugurated by Tilson Thomas. Christopher Keene was appointed Music Director. While Artpark was not to become the summer home envisioned by Krips, it did return opera to the local music scene, and the BPO performed there many times over the ensuing decades.

Original 1978 LP release of Gershwin's *Broadway Overtures* by Columbia Records.

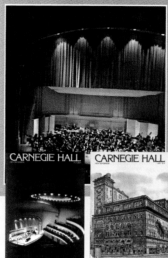

Program covers from the BPO concert series in Carnegie Hall under Michael Tilson Thomas.

DVD of the film *Manhattan* by Woody Allen, featuring the BPO on the soundtrack.

Original LP of the BPO performing the music of Carl Ruggles under the baton of Michael Tilson Thomas.

The Orchestra continued its mission as Buffalo's cultural ambassador with a variety of tours from New England to Florida. Most notably, however, the BPO returned to Carnegie Hall in 1973, and proceeded to make regular appearances there for the next six years – 12 concerts in all under Tilson Thomas' baton. The BPO also performed at Kennedy Center in Washington, DC on November 18, 1974, which the "Voice of America" taped for transmission abroad, as well as in Boston's venerable Symphony Hall in November 1979.

During the tenure of Tilson Thomas, the BPO made, among others, two LP recordings with CBS

The BPO performs a concert at M&T Plaza during the summer of 1973. Melvin Strauss is conducting.

Masterworks, including the music of Carl Ruggles and a brilliant set of Gershwin show overtures. The recording became a bestseller nationwide, featuring the concert overtures to Gershwin's *Girl Crazy*, *Of Thee I Sing*, *Let 'Em Eat Cake*, *Oh Kay*, *Funny Face* and *Strike Up the Band*, all brilliantly scored by arranger Don Rose. A few months after the recording was issued, the Buffalo Philharmonic received a request from Woody Allen to use tracks from the new LP for the background score of his upcoming film, *Manhattan*, released in 1979. Each BPO musician received a check for an extra recording session that would never take place. Allen simply used the original master tapes that had been made in Kleinhans. Part of the film score is also

continued on page 70

ARTPARK

The concept was initiated by Josef Krips in 1960 as the summer home of the Buffalo Philharmonic. A decade later, Lukas Foss participated in the groundbreaking. Finally, Michael Tilson Thomas conducted the gala grand opening of Artpark in 1974. This magnificent venue overlooking the grand Niagara Gorge was 15 years in the making, and well worth it.

On a perfect summer evening, July 25, 1974, the Artpark Theater was dedicated with a program of music and dance hosted by Cicely Tyson and James Coco. Under the baton of BPO music director Tilson Thomas, the very first pieces performed were the Canadian national anthem, *O Canada*, followed by *The Star Spangled Banner*.

The program included music from every genre for which the Artpark Theater was conceived, including orchestral masterworks, opera and American musical theater.

The BPO played from the orchestra pit for parts of the program, a role which would prove vital to the success of ballet and opera at Artpark in the coming years.

After closing remarks in the theater, the audience and Orchestra moved out to the spacious grounds where the Buffalo Philharmonic performed Tchaikovsky's *1812 Overture* in counterpoint to the perfectly

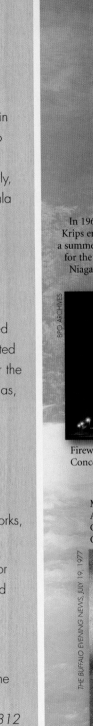

An architectural model of Artpark created for the 1970 groundbreaking.

Lukas Foss with New York Governor Rockefeller and Senator Brydges on May 14, 1970 at the groundbreaking of the performing arts center that would become Artpark. The BPO performed Ravel's *Daphnis and Chloe* Suite No. 2.

In 1960, Josef Krips envisions a summer home for the BPO in Niagara Falls.

Fireworks at the Artpark Dedication Concert on July 25, 1974.

Martha Graham and Aaron Copland at Artpark on July 13-17, 1977. The Martha Graham Dance Company performed Copland's *Appalachian Spring*.

Ballet star Edward Villella performed at the Artpark Dedication Concert.

1985 Artpark International Festival poster

Christopher Keene, Artpark Music Director, 1975-88

June 4
A STRING OF PEARLS
OPENING NIGHT GALA
PEARL BAILEY and the LOUIE BELLSON QUARTET with Raymond Harvey conducting the Philharmonic.
A sparkling opening night of favorite melodies by the inimitable songstress. Join benefit patrons for an elegant champagne and strawberry post-concert reception at the Niagara Falls Country Club ($25 includes concert and reception tickets, these available only through the Philharmonic box office).

June 6
MEGA MUSIC!
AUDIO-VISUAL FANTASY
Erich Kunzel conducts the Philharmonic with Canadian pianist William Tritt. Laser light shows, fireworks, spaceships, large-screen slide shows, and 20-foot-high-dancers are among the special effects produced to blockbuster musical favorites.

Artpark '83
Lewiston, New York

June 7
VIVA VIVALDI
(BACH, HANDEL AND MOZART, TOO!)
Buffalo's Ars Nova Musicians Chamber Orchestra and Toronto's Mainly Mozart Chamber Orchestra in a tercentenary birthday tribute to Bach and Handel, a salute to "Amadeus" and Viva Vivaldi—all going for baroque against a period setting created for this special evening.

June 8
THE RESURRECTION
Gustav Mahler's moving Second Symphony, "The Resurrection," conducted by Semyon Bychkov in his first appearance as the Philharmonic's new Music Director. Soloists Barbara Pearson and Lili Chookasian complement Buffalo's Schola Cantorum and Toronto's Mendelssohn Choir to create the grand sound (300 voices) the composer envisioned for this unique work, but is rarely performed on this scale.

All Concerts at 8:00 pm

New York City Center Ballet Company program.

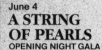
NYCB
New York City Ballet

the First...
INTERNATIONAL FESTIVAL
W·E·E·K
The Buffalo Philharmonic in resid
at Artpark

June 28 through August 28

Program cover for Wagner's *Ring*, June 27, 1985.

THE RING OF THE NIBELUNGS
(concert highlights)

8 pm August 5, 6

Artpark Theater

Music and Text by Richard Wagner
With the Buffalo Philharmonic Orchestra
Conducted by Christopher Keene

Cast
(in order of appearance)

Woglinde	Rachel Lewis
Wellgunde	Frances Webb
Flosshilde	Margery Teda
Donner	Charles Roe
Wotan	Richard Cross
Loge	Melvyn Novick
Siegmund	Robert Rue
Sieglinde	Doris Jung
Helmwige	Marilyn Brustadt
	Terri Thompson

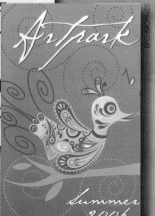
Artpark
Summer 2006

---

timed boom of cannons, followed by a spectacular fireworks display on both sides of the Niagara River. It was a night transfigured.

Artistic guidance over those remarkable early years was provided by Artpark music director Christopher Keene, who worked very closely with the BPO management and musicians, featuring the Buffalo Philharmonic in hundreds of events.

The BPO was also formally "in-residence" at Artpark for several summer seasons, offering festive Fourth of July programs with fireworks over the gorge, Viennese Nights and many Pops specials.

Artpark also brought opera back to the region, in short supply since the demise of the Zorah Berry Series.

One of the most ambitious Artpark endeavors was the complete presentation of Wagner's *Der Ring des Nibelungen* (*Ring Cycle*) under Keene's baton.

Keene was central to the success of Artpark. Fiscal realities meant that rehearsal time was always limited, yet Keene somehow seemed to get 90 minutes out of every hour.

In the late 1980s and early 1990s, New York State budget cuts brought reductions in the number of BPO events at Artpark, thus limiting the offerings of opera, ballet and modern dance with the Orchestra in the theater pit. However, the tradition of classics and sparkling Pops concerts at Artpark was rekindled by JoAnn Falletta.

Neville Mariner, guest conductor on October 19, 1974.

Michel Legrand, Hollywood composer and pianist, performed with the BPO Pops in October 1978.

Famous pianist Artur Rubinstein performed at a BPO benefit recital in Kleinhans on January 26, 1972.

Michael Tilson Thomas and Isaac Stern backstage in Kleinhans on April 23, 1972.

Itzhak Perlman performed the Tchaikovsky Violin Concerto with the BPO and Tilson Thomas on April 9, 1972.

Sarah Vaughan performed the songs of Gershwin and Bernstein in an unforgettable Pops concert on October 10, 1975 under the baton of Tilson Thomas.

continued from page 67

provided by the New York Philharmonic, and both orchestras are acknowledged in the film credits at the end of the movie.

Major soloists who appeared with the Buffalo Philharmonic during the Tilson Thomas years include violinists Itzhak Perlman and Isaac Stern; pianists Misha Dichter, Christoph Eschenbach and Artur Rubinstein; and soprano Jessye Norman.

For a Gala Pops concert on October 10, 1975 Tilson Thomas directed the Orchestra in a performance of Gershwin songs featuring jazz great Sarah Vaughan. Vaughan was invited to perform with Tilson Thomas and the BPO at Carnegie Hall in February 1976 in a repeat performance of the Buffalo concert which had been broadcast by WBEN radio and taped for the BPO Archive.*

A BPO 1974-75 season advertisement, featuring Michael Tilson Thomas – in French!

Celebrity Pops programs with Henry Mancini, Michel Legrand and Art Garfunkel brought favorite tunes and sweet memories to mind from favorite movies and bundled love letters.

One of the most lighthearted BPO events during this era was the benefit concert presented by Bob Hope in Memorial Auditorium. More than 5,000 people attended to hear the comedian's easy banter with the BPO. It was a hot August evening in 1978 and people were fanning themselves with their programs. "You're not saying go away, are you? When do you have good weather here?" quipped Hope. He sang *This is my Favorite City*, conducted by Geoffrey Clarkson, his own music director. After singing *Thanks for the Memories*, Hope asked for a chair, received a couch,

*This Sarah Vaughan performance is featured on the *BPO at 75* five-CD Anniversary set.

Folk singer Art Garfunkel performed with the BPO Pops in 1978.

Hollywood film composer Henry Mancini performed with the BPO Pops in 1976.

"Flack is Beautiful" featured Roberta Flack with the BPO on March 18, 1977.

Catch a Rising Star—In Buffalo

buffalo pops

Presents
MITCH MILLER
Conductor
Friday, November 19, 1971 – 8:30 p.m.
Kleinhans Music Hall

buffalo philharmonic pops
FRIDAY, OCTOBER 18 – 8:30 p.m.
KLEINHANS MUSIC HALL

Ella Fitzgerald sang with the BPO in a benefit concert for Buffalo General Hospital on December 6, 1974.

IGOR PRINCE

reclined and sang *I'm Lazy*. It was a memorable evening, and the funds raised were much appreciated.

More than 280 youth concerts took place during the 1970s. Tilson Thomas came to the BPO as a youth himself at 27 years old, but had the wisdom to reach beyond the podium to develop educational experiences for many levels of listeners, including exciting music and the stories behind the music, to make concerts come alive and be remembered. One of the musicians once

> ONE OF THE MUSICIANS ONCE COMMENTED THAT TILSON THOMAS WAS VERY QUIET, ALMOST SHY, ONE-ON-ONE; THAT HE WAS BETTER IN FRONT OF 300 PEOPLE; BUT THAT HE WAS AT THE TOP OF HIS GAME BEFORE OF AN AUDIENCE OF 3,000.

commented that Tilson Thomas was very quiet, almost shy, one-on-one; that he was better in front of 300 people; but that he was at the top of his game before of an audience of 3,000.

Tilson Thomas delivered some of the most memorable pre-concert lectures in the history of the orchestra, singing or playing the piano to bring even subtle concepts to light for an eager audience. His lecture-demo on Bartók's *Miraculous Mandarin* to 3,000 spell-bound and frightened students at UB in the

My grandfather was Igor Prince. He played violin in the 1st and 2nd violin sections and retired in 1975. Before concerts on school field trips to Kleinhans in the 1970s, I used to run up the stairs next to the stage to say hello to my grandfather. It made me feel very special.

As a teenager, I frequently attended BPO concerts with my grandparents after my grandfather's retirement. Michael Tilson Thomas was on the podium during one concert which stands out clearly. The last piece on the program was a late Mozart Symphony. At its conclusion, my grandfather, a man of few words, leaned over to me and said, "That was good." Then the maestro appeared to be giving us an encore. He asked the orchestra to repeat the last movement of the symphony. Then – strangest of all – he SAT DOWN on the podium! I had never seen a full orchestra play without a conductor and it was quite a sight to behold. All eyes of the players were focused on the sheet musician front of them. It made me realize how frequently the players glance up at the conductor for guidance. And, hearing the Mozart twice in a row was such a treat! The musicians, with the music fresh in their ears and in their fingers, completely held their own, even without a conductor. My grandmother whispered, "He's clever."

- DENISE PRINCE

STEINBERG RETURNS TO THE BPO

In the second week of March in 1977, William Steinberg guest conducted the BPO. Backstage, Steinberg's assistant patiently, gently assisted the maestro with his sweater. I entered the dressing room and greeted the maestro after not having seen him for 20 years, and gave him the scores he would use for the rehearsal. Several staff members slowly followed us on-stage. A few stood quietly off to the side near the stage door, Maestro Tilson Thomas among them. They were there to observe. Then, a transformation occurred which I will never forget. This frail, small man became the conductor he had always been – sharp, powerful, commanding and inspired. The musicians responded in kind. The rehearsal was as thrilling as the concert, which held the audience in thrall. More than 2,800 patrons stood to commemorate a great conductor, a great orchestra and the great musical heritage of the City of Buffalo.

- JULIUS KOVACH, ORCHESTRA LIBRARIAN

Bob Hope performed at a BPO benefit in Memorial Auditorium on August 16, 1978.

BPO bassist Frank Primerano demonstrates the string bass to students at a Kinder Konzert in 1978.

KINDER KONZERT

Philharmonic's SOS Answered

Edwin Polokoff, chairman of the Orchestra's critical $1 million fund drive in 1974, engaged the entire Western New York community to ensure success – from football to bake sales. The Buffalo Bills donated box seats and Smallwood Elementary School students in Eggertsville baked gingerbread cookies.

fall of 1977 remains etched in many alumni memories.

In September 1976, the BPO went on a major tour through seven states. A strike that would have prematurely ended the tour was narrowly avoided. However, by 1977, the strike was begun after the board proposed cutting 12 players and nine weeks from the season.

Political cartoon by Pat Cunningham featuring Michael Tilson Thomas.

The players remained on strike for a full two months. Negotiation tactics would change from then on.

Funding tactics would also change. A larger, more diverse audience was courted. Buttons, quilts and SNAPpy events (SNAP was the acronym for Saturday Night At the Philharmonic) were some of the marketing tactics employed.

CHAPTER 8

THE RUDEL YEARS

1979-1985

JULIUS RUDEL

BORN
March 6, 1921
Vienna, Austria

STUDIED
Piano, conducting and composition

FIRST BPO CONCERT
February 7 & 9, 1971 (guest conductor)
Haydn - *Symphony No.95 in C minor*
Boccherini - *Cello Concerto in B-flat major*
    Leslie Parnas, cellist
Beethoven - *The Creatures of Prometheus: Overture*
Prokofiev - *Symphony No.3 in C minor*

LAST CONCERT AS MUSIC DIRECTOR
May 17 & 18, 1985
La Montaine - *Jubilant Overture, op.20*
Rachmaninoff - *Piano Concerto No.2 in C minor, op.18*
    André Watts, pianist
Saint-Saëns - *Symphony No.3 in C minor, op.78 "Organ Symphony"*
    James Bigham, organist

RETURN BPO ENGAGEMENTS
March 13 & 14, 1987
May 5 & 6, 1990
April 13 & 14, 2002

BPO ARCHIVES

BUFFALO HIGHLIGHTS
- 19 Gala performances including Beverly Sills and Plácido Domingo
- West Coast Tour, including San Francisco and Los Angeles
- CBS Masterworks recording of holiday music

CAREER HIGHLIGHTS
- First Music Director of the Kennedy Center
- First Music Director of Wolf Trap
- Grammy Award and several nominations
- Chevalier des Arts et Lettres – France
- Has directed many of the world's finest opera companies including the Metropolitan in New York, Teatro Colón in Buenos Aires, Lyric Opera of Chicago, Opéra Bastille in Paris, Royal Opera in Copenhagen, Berlin's Deutsche Oper and the Stadttheater in Berne, Switzerland

"The sound of the Buffalo Philharmonic is only one of the remarkable aspects of its music-making.
Equally impressive is the clarity with which it plays, admirably demonstrated in the program chosen by maestro Rudel."

- THE SACRAMENTO UNION, OCTOBER 28, 1981, DURING THE WEST COAST TOUR

THE RUDEL YEARS

1979-1985

BPO MUSICIANS 1979-1980

VIOLIN I
Charles Haupt, Concertmaster
Harry Taub
Rivka Mandelkern
Marylouise Nanna
Dennis Piwowarski
Clementina Fleshler
Matthew Tworek
Frances Kaye
Marie Yadzinski
Douglas Cone
Ansgarius Aylward
Karen Farrar
Zola Cirulli
Deborah Greitzer
Carolyn Gadiel
Diana Sachs
Igor Prince

VIOLIN II
Marilynn Kregal
Julius Kovach
Philip Teibel

Jeffrey Jones
Frances Piwowarski
Donald McCrorey
Linda Fischer
Irena Coumont
Richard Kay
Diane Melillo
Lois Carson
Susan Harbison
Sheryl Krohn
Melanie Gugala

VIOLA
Laurie Kennedy
Inti Marshall
Frank Reilly
Marcia Bettigole
Harold Nissenson
Bernard Fleshler
Elizabeth Phillips
Diane Williams
Penny Anderson

CELLO
James Kennedy
Takeshi Mineta
Robert Carapetyan
Monte Hoffman
Alta Mayer
Mary Sue Wells
Constance Miller
Alden Ring
Dona Vellek

STRING BASS
Theodor Mayer
Roger Macchiaroli
William Burns
Frank Primerano
John Haas
Makoto Michii
Nicholas Molfese
Alan Yanofsky

FLUTE
John Burgess
Cheryl Gobbetti
Laurence Trott

PICCOLO
Lawrence Trott

OBOE
Rodney Pierce
Colin Smith
Florence Myers

ENGLISH HORN
Florence Myers

CLARINET
James Pyne
Daniel Johnston
Edward Yadzinski

E-FLAT CLARINET
Daniel Johnston

BASS CLARINET AND SAXOPHONE
Edward Yadzinski

BASSOON
Nelson Dayton
John Hunt
Ronald Daniels

CONTRABASSOON
Ronald Daniels

FRENCH HORN
Roy Waas
Duane Saetveit
Lowell Shaw
Fred Bradford
Milton Kicklighter

TRUMPET
David Kuehn
Charles Lirette
Gerald Soffer
Charles Gleaves

TROMBONE
Richard Myers
Fred Halt

BASS TROMBONE
Donald Miller

TUBA
Don Harry

TIMPANI
Jesse Kregal

PERCUSSION
Lynn Harbold
John Rowland

HARP
Suzanne Thomas

NOTABLE GUEST CONDUCTORS

Aaron Copland, guest conductor | April 13 & 15, 1980

Christopher Keene, guest conductor | December 9 & 11, 1979

Lukas Foss, guest conductor, pianist | January 10 & 13, 1981

Jorge Mester, guest conductor | October 17 & 20, 1981

Gunther Schuller, guest conductor | January 30 & February 2, 1982

Maxim Shostakovich, guest conductor | November 6 & 9, 1982

Stanislaw Skrowaczewski, guest conductor | April 3 & 4, 1982

John Williams, guest conductor | November 26 & 27, 1983

Gerard Schwarz, guest conductor | March 3 & 4, 1984

Yoel Levi, guest conductor | March 24 & 25, 1984

Eduardo Mata, guest conductor | February 23 & 24, 1985

Catherine Comet, guest conductor | March 8 & 9, 1985

NOTABLE GUEST SOLOISTS

Ilana Vered, pianist | October 21 & 23, 1979

Charles Haupt, violinist | January 6 & 8, 1980

Emanuel Ax, pianist | January 26 & 27, 1980

Claudio Arrau, pianist | February 3 & 5, 1980

David Golub, pianist | March 9 & 11, 1980

Jorge Bolet, pianist | March 29 & 30, 1980

Clamma Dale, soprano | April 26 & 27, 1980

André Watts, pianist | October 4 & 5, 1980

Ted Joselson, pianist | October 18 & 21, 1980

Rudolf Firkusny, pianist | November 1 & 2, 1980

Horacio Gutierrez, pianist | December 6 & 9, 1980

Kun Woo Paik, pianist | January 3 & 4, 1981

Alexis Weissenburg, pianist | March 14 & 17, 1981

Isaac Stern, violinist | October 3 & 4, 1981

John Browning, pianist | October 17 &20, 1981

Lorin Hollander, pianist | January 23 & 24, 1982

Ilana Vered, pianist | February 13 & 16, 1982

Michael Ponti, pianist | April 3 & 4, 1982

Eugene Istomin, pianist | April 17 & 20, 1982

Emanuel Ax, pianist | May 1 & 2, 1982

Ruggiero Ricci, violinist | October 16 & 19, 1982

Alexis Weissenberg, pianist | October 30 & 31, 1982

Cho-Liang Lin, violinist | December 4 & 7, 1982

Malcolm Frager, pianist | January 8 & 9, 1983

Lucy Shelton, soprano | January 22 & 25, 1983

Nadja Salerno-Sonnenberg, violinist | February 5 & 6, 1983

Ruth Laredo, pianist | February 26 & 27, 1983

Maureen Forrester, contralto | March 19 & 20, 1983

Yo-Yo Ma, cellist | April 23 & 24, 1983

Yefim Bronfman, pianist | April 30 & May 3, 1983

Leonard Pennario, pianist | May 14 & 17, 1983

Itzhak Perlman, violinist | May 20, 1983

Elmar Oliveira, violinist | October 1 & 2, 1983

Carol Wincenc, flutist | November 26 & 27, 1983

Charles Haupt, violinist | January 10, 1984

Garrick Ohlsson, pianist | February 4 & 5, 1984

André, Michel Schub, pianist | February 18 & 21, 1984

Bella Davidovich, pianist | March 9 & 10, 1984

James Vandemark, double bassist | March 24 & 25, 1984

Jeffrey Kahane, pianist | April 28 & 29, 1984

Clamma Dale, soprano | September 15 & 18, 1984

Cho-Liang Lin, violinist | February 8 & 9, 1985

Leon Fleisher, pianist | April 12 & 13, 1985

CHAIRMEN OF THE BPO BOARD OF DIRECTORS

1979 Mr. G. Wayne Hawk

1980 Mr. John B. Fisher

1981 Mr. Wayne D. Wisbaum

1982 Mr. Bedie N. Joseph

1983 Mr. Anthony Colucci

1984 Mr. Robert D. Gioia

1985 Mr. Gary L. Mucci

THE RUDEL YEARS

1979-1985

As local, national and world events continued to spin, Buffalo businesses and people spun away from the city toward the suburbs. The Tralfamadore Jazz Club opened in the theater district in an effort to draw people downtown, while SUNY at Buffalo built Slee Recital Hall and Baird Music Hall to draw people to the suburbs.

Dollar déjà vu has been on the set for years in the BPO's history. And just as a financial dilemma preceded the arrival of Michael Tilson Thomas eight years earlier, in 1978 the BPO was still recovering from the angst of a player strike just as the search for a new maestro began. Part of the spin-off from the settled strike was that the BPO board had to restructure itself, with pressure from citizen groups determined "to set things right."

At the same time, a new maestro would have to possess the gravitas and savvy needed to take on the podium of an orchestra that was at once "old-world/new-world" in heritage and reputation. The BPO had reached traditional maturity under Steinberg and Krips, but had also spread its wings over the heights of the avant-garde, piloted by Foss and Tilson Thomas.

Fortunately the BPO players and the new board saw eye-to-eye, recognizing that one of the Orchestra's long-term guest conductors was perfect for the job. In 1979, the podium of the Buffalo Philharmonic was assigned to Julius Rudel, the highly-regarded maestro of the New York City

Julius Rudel brought the BPO on a West Coast Tour just two years after his appointment as music director. Good reviews followed the orchestra.

Opera. Though faced with sobering financial limits, Rudel's tenure was marked by an emphasis on the classical repertoire as well as gala performances with major stars of the operatic stage, including Plácido Domingo and Beverly Sills.

One of Rudel's first efforts was an immensely successful Fund Drive concert. On September 15, 1979, television star Tony Randall and opera legend Robert Merrill appeared with the BPO and Rudel in a two-hour subscription telethon called "Super Band" before a live audience in Kleinhans Music Hall. Randall remarked: "It's something I've got to do. Actors can do something few people can do – raise money." And that's just what they did. More than 750 new subscribers called during those two hours alone. The musical smorgasboard included classical, pops, jazz, disco, children's favorites and marches. Phones were set up in the lobby, and interviews were taped by WIVB-TV between musical pieces. The quote that captured the fun-filled spirit of the day was by Executive Director Michael Bielski who lightly asked Randall: "Why did you come here?" "I was asked," Randall smiled. "I'll go anywhere for a free meal."

continued on page 79

OPERA

Opera is a glittering combination of drama, costume, visual glamour and glorious music. It is like no other art form.

The half-century spanning the 1870s through the 1920s was a Golden Age of Opera. Fifty years later, opera on the stage of Kleinhans Music Hall remains among the many memories of audiences who witnessed the magic of Julius Rudel, Beverly Sills and Plácido Domingo during two unforgettable Gala benefit performances.

On October 30, 1979, soprano Beverly Sills performed Mozart's *Exsultate Jubilate*. Sills and Rudel had worked together on hundreds of opera performances, and their artistic rapport was acknowledged by many curtain calls.

Perhaps never before in the Orchestra's history had a concert sold out in a single day. The November 7, 1980, concert with tenor Plácido Domingo opened with a riveting performance of Verdi's Overture to *La Forza del Destino* and sang the aria *La Fleur* from Bizet's *Carmen*. For his final encore, Domingo accompanied himself to *Granada*. The audience was enthralled. Even after three encores, there was a sense of heartbreak as the audience reluctantly left.

Rudel was highly respected in the opera world for his artistic mastery of poetic rubato – a requisite for leading singers and vocal ensembles. This reputation set the stage for future operatic performances under Semyon Bychkov and Christopher Keene.

On September 28, 1986, during the 50th Anniversary season, tenor Luciano Pavarotti, performed with pianist John Wustman in a recital in Kleinhans Music Hall. The program began with the classic Italian art song *Caro Mio Ben* by Giordani.

THE OPERA HOUSE

The Opera House opened at Main and Washington streets in 1862, much to the delight of the city's growing German and Italian populations.

Lush program cover for the BPO 1984-85 season reflects the lyrical selections of upcoming concerts.

PLACIDO DOMINGO
in concert
with
Buffalo Philharmonic Orchestra
Julius Rudel, *Music Director*

Friday, November 7 at 8:30 p.m.

Placido Domingo

Presented by WGR-TV2 and the Buffalo Philharmonic Orchestra

The BPO announces the November 7, 1980, performance of tenor Plácido Domingo. Never before had a BPO concert sold out in a single day.

Beverly Sills
in concert with the
Buffalo Philharmonic Orchestra

Julius Rudel
conductor

October 30, 1979

Close friends and colleagues, soprano Beverly Sills and Maestro Rudel presented a wonderful concert, almost *a pas de deux*, on October 10, 1979.

Operatic coloratura soprano Amelita Galli-Curci (*left*) and soprano Rosa Ponselle (*right*) are just two of the many opera superstars to sing in Buffalo during the 1920s and 1930s, respectively.

The Buffalo Philharmonic Orchestra presents...

Luciano Pavarotti
In Recital

Sunday, September 28, 8:30 p.m.   Kleinhans Music Hall

for the benefit of the Buffalo Philharmonic and the Niagara Council on the Arts

Tenor Luciano Pavarotti accepted the invitation to sing in a recital on September 28, 1986, on the stage of Kleinhans in a benefit concert for the BPO and the Niagara Council on the Arts.

Danny Kaye never failed to entertain Buffalo audiences with his wacky antics and wonderful music. Here he appears on the cover of *The Magazine* of *The Buffalo News* on March 14, 1982.

P.D.Q. Bach filled music halls wherever he went and Kleinhans was no different on March 2, 1984.

The unusual comedic style of Victor Borge drew audiences prepared to laugh before he uttered a word or played a note.

Comedian Tony Randall and Conductor Julius Rudel enjoy a humorous moment on stage in Kleinhans during the BPO "Super Band" telethon on September 13, 1979, which netted 750 season ticket pledges.

Julius Rudel conducting the BPO during the West Coast Tour in, 1981.

Two seasons later, "An Evening with Danny Kaye!" on March 21, 1982, offered a wildly funny, upbeat experience. It was well publicized that Kaye does not read a note of music, which made it all the more comical, fully outfitted as he was in concert tails. Kaye's "fake" musicianship was impeccable as he raised $100,000 for the BPO.

But Rudel also showed the depth of his orchestral gifts at every point along the way, highlighted by the rave reviews the BPO received on its first and only West Coast Tour. Concerts took place in Tucson and Tempe, AZ, San Francisco and Los Angeles, CA, and other western cities.

During the Rudel era, the BPO also performed in Carnegie Hall on November 16, 1980, at a gala at the Kennedy Center in Washington, DC, on February 7, 1981.

For the 1979 holiday season the BPO released the *Christmas in Concert* LP recording conducted by maestro Rudel.

During the 1979-80 season, Rudel initiated the "American Composer-Conductor Series" with Aaron Copland conducting his own music. Portions of this concert were filmed by CBS and aired during the following season.

In 1981, Rudel conducted the BPO in a tribute to Dr. Martin Luther King, Jr. broadcast in 1981 on national television. He organized a fundraising performance for the St. Philip's Boys Choir of Buffalo with the Buffalo Philharmonic. The program featured the North American premiere of *Laudate Pueri*, composed by Fr. José Mauricio Nunes-Garcia for boys choir, woodwinds, strings and soprano, contralto, tenor and bass soloists.

THE WEST COAST TOUR

"The sound of the Buffalo Philharmonic is only one of the remarkable aspects of its music-making. Equally impressive is the clarity with which it plays, admirably demonstrated in the program chosen by maestro Rudel."
The Sacramento Union, October 28, 1981

"Under Julius Rudel, the performance of the Buffalo Philharmonic in Davies Symphony Hall confirmed that this is one of the country's strongest musical ensembles."
San Francisco Chronicle, October 30, 1981

"The Buffalo Philharmonic is an admirably disciplined instrument - a mellow, well-balanced and expertly efficient group that played with security, relish and alertness to Rudel's every intention."
Los Angeles Times, November 3, 1981

BUFFALO PHILHARMONIC CHORUS

Originally the Buffalo Schola Cantorum, the Buffalo Philharmonic Chorus (BPC) was founded by Jessamine E. Long in 1937, just two years after the Philharmonic Orchestra came into existence.

Cameron Baird guided the group to prominence during its formative years, establishing it as the premier choral ensemble in Western New York.

The Chorus prospered under distinguished music directors, including Willis Page, Joseph Wincenc, Robert Beckwith, Melvin Strauss, Frederick Burgomaster and Peter Perret. From 1979 until his death in 2001, Thomas Swan led the chorus through a period of extraordinary growth.

It was under his baton in 1995 that the chorus' name was changed to the Buffalo Philharmonic Chorus to reflect the close association with the Orchestra.

PHOTOGRAPH FROM THE
BUFFALO PHILHARMONIC CHORUS

In 1986, Swan became the first recipient of the Cameron Baird Conductor's Chair. Current music director, Dr. Doreen Rao, was also so honored in 2008.

In 2007, to commemorate the BPC's 70th anniversary, the Chorus commissioned composer Randol Alan Bass to write *Passage Into Spirit* for Chorus, Soloist and Orchestra, a work inspired by the poetry of Walt Whitman, which premiered in Kleinhans in March 2007. A CD was released in 2009.

Members of the chorus joined with the Virginia Symphony Chorus in 2007 on a European singing tour of Prague, Leipzig and Berlin. The BPC returned to the Czech Republic in 2009 for a performance of Verdi's *Requiem* in the former Terezin Concentration Camp, symbolically titled Defiant Requiem. Most recently, the BPC performed the American premiere of Puccini's lost work *Cessato il suon dell'armi*.

THE BUFFALO NEWS, AUGUST 21, 1983

Buffalo's Music Men

BPO ARCHIVES

Feature article in *The Buffalo News* announcing the BPO's 1983-84 Season. (*From left*) Raymond Harvey, Maestro Rudel and Semyon Bychkov.

BPO ARCHIVES

Buffalo Philharmonic Orchestra

JAZZ

Oscar Peterson

BPO ARCHIVES

The golden throat of Mel Tormé and the BPO took the audience on a journey through reminiscences and romance in December 1982.

Oscar Peterson performed with the BPO on November 20, 1980, during an evening of memorable, toe-tapping jazz.

At the start of the 1979-80 season, maestro Rudel recorded several concerts on WNED-FM for a pilot broadcast series, including Beethoven's "*Emperor*" Concerto with Claudio Arrau. A live broadcast was also taped on January 26, 1980 featuring Rachmaninoff's Piano Concerto No.2 with soloist Emanuel Ax.*

During the Rudel years, Pops specials with conductors Mitch Miller and Eric Knight had broad appeal, complemented by featured appearances by Oscar Peterson, Mikhail Baryshnikov, P.D.Q. Bach (Peter Schickele), Ella Fitzgerald and Mel Tormé, among many others.

On November 19, 1981, under Rudel's baton, the BPO was featured at the dedication of the Baird Music Hall – Slee Concert Hall complex. The performance included the world premiere of *Quaint Events* by American composer David Del Tredici.

With ever-increasing demands to expand his role as an opera conductor in New York and Europe, Rudel chose not to extend his contract in Buffalo after the 1984-85 season. He departed with the admiration of BPO patrons and musicians alike.

In subsequent seasons, maestro Rudel returned to the BPO as a guest conductor on several occasions, including a splendid concert entitled "Night at the Paris Opera" featuring selections from Bizet's *Carmen*, Offenbach's *Tales of Hoffman* and Gounod's *Faust*.

*Featured on the *BPO at 75* five-CD Anniversary set.

CHAPTER 9

THE BYCHKOV YEARS

1985-1989

SEMYON BYCHKOV

BORN
November 30, 1952
St. Petersburg (Leningrad),
Russia (Soviet Union)

STUDIED
Piano, conducting

CURRENTLY
Chief conductor of the WDR Symphony
Orchestra Cologne in Cologne, Germany

FIRST BPO CONCERT
March 9 & 11, 1980
Beethoven - *Symphony No.8*
in F major, op.93
Grieg - *Piano Concerto in A minor, op.16*
    David Golub, pianist
Rachmaninoff - *Symphonic Dances, op.45*

LAST CONCERT AS MUSIC DIRECTOR
May 20 & 21, 1989
Brahms - *Symphony No.3 in F major, op.90*
Brahms - *Symphony No.1 in C minor,*
op.68

RETURN BPO ENGAGEMENTS
November 4 & 5, 1989
January 12 & 13, 1990

BPO ARCHIVES

BUFFALO HIGHLIGHTS
- Three Carnegie Hall appearances
- European Tour, 1988 –
  Germany, Switzerland, Austria, Italy
- 50th Anniversary Concert,
  November 16, 1985

CAREER HIGHLIGHTS
- Emigrated to the United States in 1975
- Conducted the Grand Rapids Symphony
  at the opening of the Gerald R. Ford
  Presidential Museum, July 4, 1983 at
  which he became an American citizen
- Music Director, Orchestre de Paris,
  1989-1998
- Principal Conductor, WDR Symphony
  Orchestra (Cologne), 1997-present

"The symphony orchestra is the most amazing and complex institution ever invented by humanity."

- SEMYON BYCHKOV

CHAPTER 9
THE BYCHKOV YEARS
1985-1989

BPO ARCHIVES

BPO MUSICIANS 1985-1986

VIOLIN I
Charles Haupt, Concertmaster
Harry Taub
Ansgarius Aylward
Marylouise Nanna
Clementina Fleshler
Sheryl Krohn
Matthew Tworek
Frances Kaye
Douglas Cone
Karen Soffer
Deborah Greitzer
Diana Sachs Aylward
Yakov Boroditsky
Nancy McFarland
Alan Ross

VIOLIN II
Marilynn Kregal
Julius Kovach
Philip Teibel
Jeffrey Jones
Frances Morgante

Donald McCrorey
Linda Fischer
Melanie Gugala-Haas
Richard Kay
Diane Melillo
Lois Carson
Robert Prokes

VIOLA
Benjamin Simon
Valerie Heywood
Frank Reilly
Marcia Bettigole
Harold Nissenson
Bernard Fleshler
Shuntatsu Kohno
Elizabeth Phillips
Diane Williams
André Roy

CELLO
Arie Lipsky
Eva Leininger
Nancy Anderson
Robert Carapetyan
Monte Hoffman
Robert Hausmann
Mary Sue Donavan
Constance Miller
Alden Ring
Richard Brown

STRING BASS
Roger Macchiaroli
William Burns
Frank Primerano
John Haas
Makoto Michii
Nicholas Molfese
Peter Berquist

FLUTE
John Burgess
Cheryl Gobbetti
Laurence Trott

PICCOLO
Lawrence Trott

OBOE
Rodney Pierce
Colin Smith
Florence Myers

ENGLISH HORN
Florence Myers

CLARINET
James Pyne
Daniel Johnston
Edward Yadzinski

BASS CLARINET AND SAXOPHONE
Edward Yadzinski

BASSOON
Nelson Dayton
Ronald Daniels
Martha Martin

CONTRABASSOON
Martha Martin

FRENCH HORN
Roy Waas
Duane Saetveit
Lowell Shaw
Fred Bradford
Milton Kicklighter

TRUMPET
David Kuehn
Gerald Soffer
Philip Christner
Charles Gleaves

TROMBONE
Richard Myers
Fred Halt

BASS TROMBONE
Donald Miller

TUBA
Don Harry

TIMPANI
Jesse Kregal

PERCUSSION
Lynn Harbold

HARP
Suzanne Thomas

NOTABLE GUEST CONDUCTORS

Franco Autori, guest conductor | November 16, 1985

Maxim Shostakovich, guest conductor | December 6 & 7, 1985

Christopher Keene, guest conductor | April 25 & 26, 1986

Lukas Foss, conductor | May 9 & 10, 1986

Stanislaw Skrowaczewski, guest conductor | March 22 & 23, 1986

Michael Tilson Thomas, conductor | April 19 & 20, 1986

Emmanuel Krivine, guest conductor | April 3 & 4, 1987

Jean-Pierre Rampal, flutist, guest conductor | February 13 & 14, 1987

Maximiano Valdes, conductor | October 24 & 25, 1987

Catherine Comet, guest conductor | November 6 & 7, 1987

Andrew Litton, guest conductor | October 14 & 15, 1988

John Mauceri, guest conductor | October 28 & 29, 1988

Lukas Foss, conductor | December 4 & 5, 1987

David Zinman, guest conductor | February 20 & 21, 1988

Hermann Michael, guest conductor | November 19 & 20, 1988

Hans Graf, guest conductor | March 11 & 12, 1989

Hugh Wolff, guest conductor | March 31 & April 1, 1989

Kent Nagano, guest conductor | April 15 & 16, 1989

Claus Peter Flor, guest conductor | January 14 & 15, 1988

John Nelson, guest conductor | January 27 & 28, 1989

Stanislaw Skrowaczewski, guest conductor | March 22 & 23, 1986

NOTABLE GUEST SOLOISTS

Lorin Hollander, pianist | October 11 & 12, 1985

Alicia de Larrocha, pianist | October 19 & 20, 1985

Senator Daniel Patrick Moynihan, narrator | November 16, 1985

James Galway, flutist | November 16, 1985

Roberta Peters, soprano | November 16, 1985

David Golub, pianist | November 24 & 25, 1985

Claudio Arrau, pianist | December 6 & 7, 1985

Shlomo Mintz, violinist | February 1 & 2, 1986

Joshua Bell, violinist | March 7 & 8, 1986

Murray Perahia, pianist | March 22 & 23, 1986

Isaac Stern, violinist | April 19 & 20, 1986

Leonard Pennario, pianist | April 4 & 5, 1986

Carol Wincenc, flutist | May 9 & 10, 1986

Bella Davidovich, pianist | May 17 & 18, 1986

Maurice André, trumpeter | October 25 & 26, 1986

Dimitry Sitkovetsky, violinist | November 14 & 15, 1986

Lynn Harrell, cellist | January 16 & 17, 1987

Nigel Kennedy, violinist | January 31 & February 1, 1987

Gary Graffman, pianist | March 13, 1987

Christopher Parkening, guitarist | April 3 & 4, 1987

Saul Elkin, narrator | May 16 & 17, 1987

Rudolf Firkusny, pianist | May 16 & 17, 1987

Cho-Liang Lin, violinist | September 12 & 13, 1987

David Geringas, cellist | September 25 & 26, 1987

Andrea Lucchesini, pianist | October 16 & 17, 1987

Maureen Forrester, contralto | October 24 & 25, 1987

John Browning, pianist | November 6 & 7, 1987

Peter Serkin, pianist | November 28 & 29, 1987

Jeffrey Kahane, pianist | January 16 & 17, 1988

Anne-Sophie Mutter, violinist | January 29 & 30, 1988

Andras Schiff, pianist | February 20 & 21, 1988

Charles Haupt, violinist | April 25 & 26, 1986

Claudia Hoca, pianist | May 14 & 15, 1988

Richard Stoltzman, clarinetist | May 20 & 21, 1988

Marielle Labeque, pianist | September 24 & 25, 1988

Katia Labeque, pianist | September 24 & 25, 1988

Sergei Edelmann, pianist | November 19 & 20, 1988

Emanuel Ax, pianist | November 25 & 26, 1988

Benita Valente, soprano | January 14 & 15, 1988

André Watts, pianist | January 27 & 28, 1989

John McLaughlin, guitarist | February 17 & 18, 1989

Midori, violinist | March 31 & April 1, 1989

CHAIRMEN OF THE BPO BOARD OF DIRECTORS

1985 Mr. Gary L. Mucci   1986 Mr. J. William Morris   1987-1990 Mr. Wilfred J. Larson

THE BYCHKOV YEARS

1985-1989

As Buffalo rallied to support cultural organizations struggling financially, the business community helped make the city shine. Two projects in particular were the restorations of the Butler Mansion on Delaware Avenue, and of the Market Arcade Complex on Main Street. Both buildings were designed with celebrations in mind; the former for the social elite, the latter for lighthearted shoppers and diners – perfect venues to visit before and after concerts.

When Semyon Bychkov was named to succeed Julius Rudel as BPO music director, a whirlwind of excitement ensued. Bychkov was a dynamic young Russian émigré with an irrepressible style, both personally and musically. He had served as the BPO's principal guest conductor for the previous four seasons, after two seasons as Rudel's hand-picked associate conductor.

At the same time, Bychkov had already been singled out by the European press as a top candidate for the helm of several major orchestras. Indeed, perhaps with an eventual eye on one of those prestigious appointments, Bychkov made it clear that a condition of his acceptance of the Buffalo post was that the BPO make every effort to schedule the Orchestra's first European tour during his tenure.

During his 10 seasons with the BPO, Bychkov made many close friends, in the orchestra as well as in the community. He charmed the town when he sold *The Buffalo News* on Kids Day, and nobody had a greater passion for

Semyon Bychkov conducting a BPO rehearsal.

chicken wings than Bychkov. He admitted that as soon as he steps off an airplane in Buffalo, he heads straight for home with a chicken wing detour, "medium hot, please."

For Bychkov, taking on the BPO was a gambit well-played, but not in the least a gamble. With regard to a possible tour abroad, he knew full well that the BPO would make a stellar impression in the great concert halls in Europe.

Many world-class performers and guest conductors came to Buffalo during the Bychkov years. Among the most distinguished was Luciano Pavarotti, who performed a benefit concert for the BPO and the Niagara Council on the Arts on September 28, 1986, in Kleinhans Music Hall.

Bychkov had a strong commitment to the primary orchestral repertoire. At the same time, the BPO stayed in step and in tune with Pops concerts and special programs like the Stained Glass series, in which the Orchestra performed in dozens of churches and temples throughout Western New York.

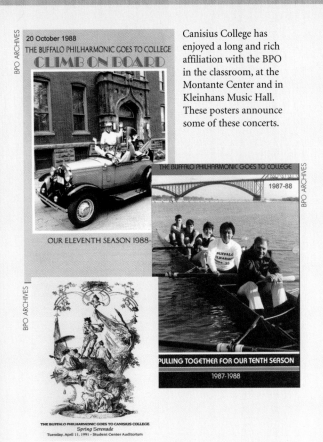

Canisius College has enjoyed a long and rich affiliation with the BPO in the classroom, at the Montante Center and in Kleinhans Music Hall. These posters announce some of these concerts.

The European Tour season is commemorated by this 1988-89 BPO Season calendar.

Appointed staff conductor in 1985, Paul Ferrington is still with the BPO in its 75th Anniversary season.

The Amherst Saxophone Quartet, seated with jazz great Eubie Blake, soloed with the BPO in 1985.

Eric Kunzel was named Principal Pops conductor in 1985, the first ever appointed by the BPO.

Sunday Brunch concerts were also very popular under the sing-along baton of Mitch Miller, as were the Fisher-Price Family Concerts, including a Sesame Street Special with Bob McGrath.

As the newly appointed Principal Pops Conductor, Eric Kunzel initiated the "Beer & Jeans" concerts with a street-savvy, up-beat repertoire. Various Pops concerts featured a host of well-known performers including Richard Hayman, Oscar Peterson and Marvin Hamlisch, among many others.

About 80 Youth Concerts were presented by the BPO during the Bychkov era. A diverse repertoire was programmed in two tiers, grades K-6 and 7-12, conducted by Raymond Harvey and Arie Lipsky. Of particular note was "Fantasy Tales," devoted to great legends and myths told through music, including *Hansel and Gretel*, *Peer Gynt* and *Firebird*.

The brilliance of the BPO under Bychkov's baton may best be represented by the splendid CD of Symphony No.5 by Shostokovich.* The recording was taped during a live performance just two weeks before the Orchestra left

*Featured on the *BPO at 75* five-CD Anniversary set.

PHOTO BY TIMOTHY WHITE

Joshua Bell performed the Bruch Violin Concerto No.1 on March 7, 1986.

BPO ARCHIVES

Midori performed the Paganini Violin Concerto No.1 on October 18, 1986.

PHOTOGRAPH FROM VASILEVA

Maxim Shostakovich guest conducted the BPO on December 6, 1985. The program featured Debussy's *Trois Nocturnes*, Beethoven's Piano Concerto No.3 in C minor and Prokofiev's Symphony No.7 in C-sharp minor.

BPO ARCHIVES

BPO 50TH ANNIVERSARY

"Opening night was a night when hopes ran high that the BPO may be on the road to international status. It was a night anything seemed possible. There was a heady rush of walking by the high-intensity projections of the orchestra's logo on Kleinhans' outside walls, or walking past the television lights and formally clad patrons in the lobby.

For at least one night, Bychkov's dream of making attendance at Philharmonic concerts the 'must thing to do' came true. Kleinhans Music Hall, radiating the Philharmonic's highest hopes of a new era that could elevate the entire city, *was* the place to be."

- CHARLES ANZALONE
The Buffalo News, Sunday, September 22, 1985

on its first European Tour, which featured several performances of the work.

Within just a few short weeks after the BPO returned to Buffalo from Europe, it was announced that Bychkov had been lured from his Buffalo post by the Orchestre de Paris. Of course there were patrons and musicians alike who were disappointed that Bychkov decided to

HE CHARMED THE TOWN WHEN HE SOLD *THE BUFFALO NEWS* ON KIDS DAY, AND NOBODY HAD A GREATER PASSION FOR CHICKEN WINGS THAN BYCHKOV.

move on so abruptly, especially after the community had rallied in support of the European tour and the Orchestra had performed so brilliantly, not only in Europe but also in Carnegie Hall and in Kleinhans. But community pride soon won the day, and Bychkov and the Orchestra kept the game high during his fourth and final season in 1988-89.

BPO ON TOUR

As Buffalo's cultural ambassador, the BPO has toured throughout the greater part of its 75-year history. More than 350 cities have opened their concert curtains to present the Buffalo Philharmonic across the USA, Canada and Europe.

THE EUROPEAN TOUR

When it was announced that the young and brilliant Semyon Bychkov would become the BPO's eighth music director, efforts began immediately to send the BPO on a European tour. The first tour of European concert halls in the Orchestra's history was confirmed by the Board of Directors just eight months later.

Two years of planning were needed to make it all play out smoothly. In the second week of April 1988, a cargo jet left the Buffalo Niagara International Airport bound for Frankfurt, Germany, loaded with the Orchestra's larger instruments, all in bulky, jet-worthy cases. Bon voyage!

The BPO musicians followed a day later, with the first concert at Frankfurt's Alten Oper on April 12, 1988. The itinerary took the Orchestra to Germany, Austria, Switzerland and Italy.

Thomas Angian, director of the Musikverein, expressed amazement that, with less than an hour to rehearse, the BPO and Bychkov were able to adapt so well to the acoustics of the Hall. "It's the most un-American American orchestra I've ever heard." Something must have sounded right. Bychkov was signed as the new music director of the Orchestre de Paris just a few weeks later.

European Tour program covers

2010 Florida Friends
Tour announcements

Program covers from tours to
Carnegie Hall, Troy Music Hall
and Louise M. Davies Symphony
Hall in San Francisco.

Celebrating the BPO's
75th Anniversary
**The Florida
Friends Tour**
March 2010

Lukas Foss toured the
Eastern Seaboard with pianist
Charles Rosen in April 1966.

The BPO toured with Arthur Fiedler
as the "Boston Pops" for one season
in 1964. The next season they toured
again with Fiedler, but as the Buffalo
Pops Orchestra.

U.S. AND CANADIAN TOURS

The Orchestra's earliest documented tour was
in December 1949, with an itinerary that
included Pennsylvania, New York and several
New England states under the baton of
William Steinberg. Under Josef Krips, the
BPO visited more than 75 cities in 13 states,
including concerts in Ontario, Quebec and
the Maritime Provinces.

The most active tour schedule in the BPO's
history took place during the Foss years. In all,
156 tour dates were filled, including two Pops
tours under Arthur Fiedler. The Orchestra also
played for the first time in Carnegie Hall and
Lincoln Center in New York, and was featured
during Expo '67 in Montreal's Place des Arts.

Although the cost of touring rose sharply in
the Michael Tilson Thomas years, the BPO
made tours to New England and Florida, with
appearances at Boston's Symphony Hall and
Kennedy Center in Washington, DC. Under
Tilson Thomas, the Orchestra also established
its own Carnegie Hall series, offering a dozen
concerts between 1974 and 1979.

Julius Rudel directed the BPO on its first West
Coast Tour, with rave reviews from the press.
Rudel also took the Orchestra to Carnegie
Hall and Kennedy Center.

Financial constraints kept the BPO off the
touring circuit during the tenure of Maximiano
Valdes. When JoAnn Falletta was appointed
Music Director in 1998, the BPO had not
toured for a decade, although possibilities
began to develop. The BPO returned to
Carnegie Hall for two concerts in 2004
and made a successful Florida Friends
Tour in 2010.

50TH ANNIVERSARY

Festival!
A Gala Birthday Celebration

BUFFALO PHILHARMONIC ORCHESTRA

FESTIVAL 50

Semyon Bychkov

Roberta Peters

The program featured guest soloists soprano Roberta Peters and flutist James Galway and Senator Daniel Patrick Moynihan. How moving it must have been to hear Senator Moynihan narrate Copland's *Lincoln Portrait.*

GOLDEN GALA

BUFFALO PHILHARMONIC ORCHESTRA
Semyon Bychkov, Music Director
November 16, 1985

Glinka
Russlan and Ludmilla: Overture

Mozart
Voi avete un cor fedele, K.217

Handel
Rinaldo: Lascia ch'io pianga

Rossini
*The Barber of Seville:
Una voce poco fa*

Rodrigo
Fantasia para un gentilehombre

Bizet/Borne
Carmen Fantasy for Flute

Bishop
Lo, Hear the Gentle Lark

de Falla
*The Three Cornered Hat:
Final Dance*

Copland
Lincoln Portrait

Mussorgsky/Ravel
Pictures at an Exhibition

BUFFALO PHILHARMONIC ORCHESTRA
50
FESTIVAL

1985-86 GOLDEN ANNIVERSARY SEASON

As a memento of the 50th Anniversary Gala, the Orchestra issued an LP featuring Mussorgsky/Ravel *Pictures at an Exhibition,* as well as other selections from the evening.

BUFFALO PHILHARMONIC ORCHESTRA
FESTIVAL

The Buffalo Philharmonic Orchestra's Gala 50th Anniversary Concert took place on November 16, 1985. Franco Autori returned to the podium as guest conductor, bringing a fitting historical touch to the celebration. The Gala also welcomed Semyon Bychkov to Buffalo as the new music director. The old and the new, celebrating a half century of beautiful music in Buffalo.

CHAPTER 10

THE VALDES YEARS

1989-1998

MAXIMIANO VALDES

BPO ARCHIVES

BORN
June 14, 1949
Santiago, Chile

STUDIED
Piano, conducting

CURRENTLY
Conductor Laureate of the Orquesta Sinfónica del Principado de Asturias in Spain; Music Director/Principal Conductor of the Puerto Rico Symphony; and Conductor Laureate, Festival Casals, San Juan

FIRST BPO CONCERT
October 24 & 25, 1987
(guest conductor, American debut)
Mozart - *Symphony No.36 in C major, K.425 "Linz"*
Mahler - *Songs of a Wayfarer*
   Maureen Forrester, contralto
Prokofiev - *Romeo and Juliet (excerpts, Suites 1, 2 and 3)*

LAST CONCERT AS MUSIC DIRECTOR
May 30 & 31, 1998
Brahms - *Concerto for Violin and Cello in A minor, op.102*
   Arie Lipsky, cellist
   Charles Haupt, violinist
Mahler - *Symphony No.5 in C-sharp minor*

RETURN BPO ENGAGEMENTS
November 22 & 23, 2003
November 15 & 16, 2008

BUFFALO HIGHLIGHTS
- Established pre-concert lectures as a BPO maestro tradition
- Conducted the BPO in many live-performance broadasts on WNED including Mozart's *"Linz" Symphony No.36*
- Conducted BPO's Kleinhans performance of Mozart's *Magic Flute*

CAREER HIGHLIGHTS
- Conducted a concert in honor of the inauguration of the President of Chile in 1990
- An impressive discography with a variety of orchestras including the Royal Philharmonic, the Monte Carlo Philharmonic, the Nice Philharmonic and the London Symphony
- First prize, Nicolai Malko Competition, Copenhagen

"After my first few minutes of rehearsal with the Buffalo Philharmonic in 1987, I was struck by a feeling that an already strong musical relationship was starting to exist between the orchestra and me."
- MAXIMIANO VALDES

CHAPTER 10
THE VALDES YEARS
1989-1998

BPO MUSICIANS 1989-1990

VIOLIN I
Charles Haupt, Concertmaster
Harry Taub
Ansgarius Aylward
Marylouise Nanna
Clementina Fleshler
Sheryl Genco
Matthew Tworek
Frances Kaye
Douglas Cone
Karen Soffer
Deborah Greitzer
Diana Sachs Aylward
Nancy Gaub
Alan Ross
Melanie Haas
Andrea Blanchard

VIOLIN II
Marilynn Kregal
Julius Kovach
Philip Teibel
Jeffrey Jones

Frances Morgante
Donald McCrorey
Richard Kay
Robert Prokes
Yu-Hui Tamae Lee
Diane Melillo
Lois Carson
Gina Feinauer
Amy Kinney

VIOLA
Chauncey Patterson
Valerie Heywood-How
Inti Marshall
Frank Reilly
Marcia Bettigole
Harold Nissenson
Elizabeth Phillips
Shuntatsu Kohno
Bernard Fleshler
Diane Williams

CELLO
Arie Lipsky
Eva Leininger
Robert Carapetyan
Nancy Anderson
Monte Hoffman
Robert Hausmann
Mary Sue Donavan
Constance Miller
Alden Ring
Joel Becktell

STRING BASS
Roger Macchiaroli
William Burns
Frank Primerano
John Haas
Makoto Michii
Nicholas Molfese

FLUTE
John Burgess
Cheryl Gobbetti
Laurence Trott

PICCOLO
Lawrence Trott

OBOE
Rodney Pierce
Colin Smith
Florence Myers

ENGLISH HORN
Florence Myers

CLARINET
Diana Haskell
Daniel Johnston
Edward Yadzinski

E-FLAT CLARINET
Daniel Johnston

BASS CLARINET AND SAXOPHONE
Edward Yadzinski

BASSOON
Nelson Dayton
Ronald Daniels
Martha Malkiewicz

CONTRABASSOON
Martha Malkiewicz

FRENCH HORN
Roy Waas
Duane Saetveit
Lowell Shaw
Scott Snowden
Milton Kicklighter

TRUMPET
David Kuehn
Gerald Soffer
Philip Christner
Charles Gleaves

TROMBONE
Richard Myers
Fred Halt

BASS TROMBONE
Donald Miller

TUBA
Don Harry

TIMPANI
Jesse Kregal

PERCUSSION
Lynn Harbold
Jack Brennan

HARP
Suzanne Thomas

NOTABLE GUEST CONDUCTORS

Kent Nagano, guest conductor | March 31 & April 1, 1990
Julius Rudel, conductor | May 5 & 6, 1990
Gregory Nowak, guest conductor | November 29 & December 1, 1990
Eiji Oue, conductor | January 31 & February 2 & 3, 1991
George Cleve, guest conductor | February 8 & 9, 1991
John Nelson, guest conductor | February 16 & 17, 1991
Salvatore Accardo, guest conductor | April 18, 20 & 21, 1991
Hermann Michael, guest conductor | November 2 & 3, 1991
Marin Alsop, guest conductor | January 11 & 12, 1992
Kazuyoshi Akiyama, guest conductor | March 13 & 14, 1992
Muhai Tang, guest conductor | April 11 & 12, 1992
Hans Graf, guest conductor | May 2 & 3, 1992
Christopher Seaman, guest conductor | October 3 & 4, 1992
Yoav Talmi, guest conductor | November 7 & 8, 1992
Lukas Foss, conductor | November 21 & 22, 1992
Kenneth Jean, guest conductor | January 8 & 9, 1993

Christopher Keene, guest conductor | January 23 & 24, 1993
Yoel Levi, guest conductor | April 24 & 25, 1993
Robert Spano, guest conductor | January 21 & 22, 1994
Sergiu Comissiona, guest conductor | November 4 & 6, 1993
Jesse Levine, guest conductor | February 25 & 26, 1994
Neal Stulberg, guest conductor | March 11 & 12, 1994
Gerard Schwarz, guest conductor | March 26 & 27, 1994
Roberto Abbado, guest conductor | May 11 & 12, 1996
Michael Christie, guest conductor | November 22 & 23, 1997
Christopher Wilkins, guest conductor | March 8 & 9, 1997
Hobart Earle, guest conductor | November 15 & 16, 1997
JoAnn Falletta, guest conductor | February 7 & 8, 1998
Carlos Kalmar, guest conductor | March 7 & 8, 1998
George Pehlivanian, guest conductor | March 21 & 22, 1998
James Paul, guest conductor | April 4 & 5, 1998
Uriel Segal, guest conductor | April 25 & 26, 1998

NOTABLE GUEST SOLOISTS

Marielle Labeque, pianist | November 4 & 5, 1989
Katia Labeque, pianist | November 4 & 5, 1989
Gyorgy Pauk, violinist | December 2 & 3, 1989
Garrick Ohlsson, pianist | January 12 & 13, 1990
André Watts, pianist | March 31 & April 1, 1990
Elmar Oliveira, violinist | April 20 & 21, 1990
Bella Davidovich, pianist | May 5 & 6, 1990
Frederica von Stade, mezzo-soprano |
   May 18 & 19, 1990
Charles Haupt, violinist | November 16 & 17, 1990
Ana-Maria Vera, pianist | January 12 & 13, 1991
Claudia Hoca, pianist | January 19 & 20, 1991
Amherst Saxophone Quartet | February 8 & 9, 1991
Horacio Gutierrez, pianist | February 16 & 17, 1991
Toby Hoffman, violist | April 18, 20 & 21, 1991
Lynn Harrell, cellist | May 2, 4 & 5, 1991
Edith Wiens, soprano | May 18 & 19, 1991
Mark Kaplan, violinist | July 5, 1991
Sergei Edelmann, pianist | July 27, 1991
Alicia de Larrocha, pianist | October 5 & 6, 1991

Pascal Rog, pianist | October 19 & 20, 1991
Carol Wincenc, flutist | January 11 & 12, 1992
Aurora Natola-Ginastera, cellist | February 29 & March 1, 1992
Tatiana Troyanos, soprano | April 11 & 12, 1992
Gustav Rivinius, cellist | May 2 & 3, 1992
Peter Donohoe, pianist | October 3 & 4, 1992
Cristina Ortiz, pianist | October 24 & 25, 1992
Nexus Percussion Quintet | October 16 & 17, 1992
Hermann Baumann, hornist | January 8 & 9, 1993
Benita Valente, soprano | January 23 & 24, 1993
Gil Shaham, violinist | March 26 & 27, 1993
Bruno Leonardo Gelber, pianist | April 3 & 4, 1993
Joshua Bell, violinist | April 24 & 25, 1993
Helene Grimaud, pianist | October 16 & 17, 1993
So-Yun Park, violinist | November 20 & 21, 1993
Pinchas Zukerman, violinist | February 4 & 5, 1994
Carter Brey, cellist | March 26 & 27, 1994
Jacques Israelievitch, violinist | April 23 & 24, 1994
Midori, violinist | April 30 & May 1, 1994
Doc Severinsen, trumpeter | October 22 & 23, 1994

Fabio Bidini, pianist | November 25 & 26, 1994
Edward Ruivenkamp, tenor | January 13 & 14, 1995
Christina Wilcox, mezzo-soprano |
   January 13 & 14, 1995
Cho-Liang Lin, violinist | March 10 & 11, 1995
Lilya Zilberstein, pianist | December 8 & 9, 1995
Orli Shaham, pianist | April 13 & 14, 1996
Leila Josefowicz, violinist | April 13 & 14, 1996
Christopher Plummer, narrator | May 24 & 25, 1996
Maxim Vengerov, violinist | October 2, 1996
Louis Lortie, pianist | October 5 & 6, 1996
Roberto Diaz, violist | February 8 & 9, 1997
Claudine Carlson, mezzo-soprano | April 5 & 6, 1997
Leon Fleisher, pianist | May 3 & 4, 1997
Sherill Milnes, baritone | September 20 & 21, 1997
Barry Douglas, pianist | October 25 & 26, 1997
Hakan Hardenberger, trumpeter | March 21 & 22, 1998
Tzimon Barto, pianist | April 25 & 26, 1998
Michala Petri, recorder | May 9 & 10, 1998

CHAIRMEN OF THE BPO BOARD OF DIRECTORS

1987-1990 Mr. Wilfred J. Larson
1991-1992 Mr. Andrew J. Rudnick
1993-1994 Mr. William L. McHugh
1995-1997 Mr. John D. Reinhold
1998 Mr. Robert M. Greene

THE VALDES YEARS

1989-1998

I n music, the era was marked by high-tech innovations including the introduction of the CD as the format of choice for recorded music, the ubiquitous boom box and the SONY Walkman. In 1990 America lost two of its most revered composers with the passing of Aaron Copland and Leonard Bernstein. And on July 7, 1990 an unlikely sporting event gave rise to the greatest selling classical album of all time: a recording of "The Three Tenors" at a special concert just before the 1990 FIFA World Cup Finals in Rome.

Following the BPO's European tour in the spring of 1988, the Orchestra was suddenly faced with the challenge of finding a new music director. Fortunately Semyon Bychkov remained to fill the fourth and final year of his contract in a season of splendid music-making, including the Orchestra's 20th appearance at Carnegie Hall on October 2, 1988.

Back in Buffalo in 1989, BPO patrons eagerly awaited news about who would be selected to fill the post of music director. During the days of Lukas Foss and Michael Tilson Thomas, the Orchestra had earned a stellar reputation for discovery and adventurous programming. And under the baton of Semyon Bychkov, the BPO had again demonstrated its artistic mettle with the big-decibel masterworks in the repertoire, Mahler and Shostakovich in particular.

MAXIMIANO VALDES, MUSIC DIRECTOR
DOC SEVERINSEN, PRINCIPAL POPS CONDUCTOR

Buffalo Philharmonic Orchestra

57th SEASON • 1992/1993

BPO ARCHIVES

A brilliant and dashing Chilean conductor named Maximiano Valdes appeared as a guest conductor with the BPO on October 24 and 25, 1987, in a program that featured Maureen Forrester singing Mahler's *Songs of a Wayfarer*. No one realized it at the time, but it was a perfect audition for Señor Valdes, who revealed his special dynamic finesse throughout the concert. The *"Linz"* Symphony of Wolfgang Amadeus Mozart was extraordinary for its vibrant poise. Valdes also conjured the haunting bravura required for Prokofiev's ballet masterpiece *Romeo and Juliet*.

For Opening Night of his first season in Buffalo, maestro Valdes chose two of the greatest ballet scores of the 20th century: Stravinsky's *Petrouchka* and Ravel's *Daphnis and Chloé*. No overtures or fanfares, no big symphony, no renowned soloists. Just the BPO

continued on page 97

BPO ARCHIVES

PHOTOGRAPH BY BRIDGITTE LACOMBE, FROM MARIELLE LABEQUE

PHOTOGRAPH BY RHEA ANNA

Duo-pianists Katia and Marielle Labeque performed Mendelssohn's Concerto for Two Pianos with the BPO on November 4, 1989.

Doc Severinsen has a very unconventional technique when he warms up to play. While virtually all brass players go through a routine of special soft tones as warm-ups. Doc is famous for doing the opposite. He lifts his trumpet to his lips and warms up with loud, roaring low tones and a few screech owl wails that sound like a motorcycle burning rubber. Amazing – because just a few moments later, he can break your heart with a sweet version of *Danny Boy* or *Body and Soul*.

Singer/songwriter Ani DiFranco performed *Amazing Grace* with the BPO under the baton of Doc Severinsen at the opening of the Marine Midland Arena on September 27, 1996.

BPO ARCHIVES

"MAX VALDES' CONCERTS ALWAYS FELT RELAXED AND ELEGANT. HIS CONNECTION TO MUSIC CAME ALMOST FROM A DANCE PERSPECTIVE WHICH ALWAYS LEFT THE AUDIENCE WITH A FIRST-RATE PERFORMANCE. REHEARSALS CAN BE SOLELY CEREBRAL WITH MANY CONDUCTORS AND BY PERFORMANCE TIME THERE IS NOTHING LEFT IN THE WELL. WITH MAX I ALWAYS FELT THAT HE WAS FOCUSED ON THE PERFORMANCE."

- DON HARRY, TUBA

1991 THE GULF WAR IN THE MIDDLE EAST   **1992** HURRICANE ANDREW HITS FLORIDA AND THE GULF COAST

PHOTOGRAPH BY RICHARD W. ROELLER/THE BUFFALO NEWS, JANUARY 25, 1990

"I believe in the intelligence of the audience," Mitch Miller is quoted as saying in a January 25, 1990 *Buffalo News* article by Herman Trotter, "and refuse to play down to them."

PHOTOGRAPH BY CORI WELLS BRAUN

Flutist Carol Wincenc, daughter of BPO conductor Joseph Wincenc, performed Mozart's Flute Concerto on January 11, 1992.

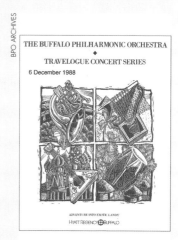

BPO ARCHIVES

Program cover from one of the Travelogue concerts held at the Buffalo Hyatt Regency Hotel during the late 1980s and early 1990s.

BPO ARCHIVES

Stained Glass concerts took place in churches and synagogues. This program was conducted by Marylouise Nanna, a member of the violin section and founder of Ars Nova, at the Full Gospel Tabernacle in April 1996.

---

performing two of the world's greatest showcase scores, each an orchestral *tour de force*. Given the concert heritage in Buffalo, it was a delightful and daring choice.

The seasons that followed were marked by Valdes' savvy eye for program variety in both the standard and contemporary repertoire, all delivered with a delectable Romantic-era touch.

Maestro Valdes also initiated an important expansion of pre-concert lectures for the Classics series. Although such lectures had been offered in the past, they were only for special events such as world premiere performances with composer interviews. Valdes presented most of the lectures himself, highlighted by his unique ability to represent

WITH HIS SILVER "TONIGHT SHOW" TRUMPET IN HAND, DOC SEVERINSEN TOOK OVER THE POPS PODIUM IN 1992. SEVERINSEN'S MANY SOLD OUT CONCERTS FEATURED LEADING POP, JAZZ AND BROADWAY SOLOISTS.

a musical phrase or motif with just a few notes at the piano. Especially effective were his demo-analyses of the music of Stravinsky and the scores of French and Spanish Impressionists, including Roussel, Debussy and Falla.

In addition to the Classics and Pops concert series, the BPO maintained the Stained Glass, Discovery and Travelog offerings. A new series called Sights, Sounds and Symphony was launched which enhanced concerts with graphic and laser effects, cued and sparked by the musical colors and rhythms produced by the Orchestra.

In 1990, the BPO awarded the Principal Pops baton to the irrepressible Mitch Miller, who had conducted the Buffalo Philharmonic over the years in performances in Kleinhans

continued on page 100

BPO AND THE SCHOOLS

Within weeks of its formation in 1935, the Buffalo Philharmonic began to deliver on one of its most important functions: to bring great music to young ears. The Buffalo Philharmonic's very first education concert took place on December 17, 1935, appropriately presented by The Music Department of the Buffalo Public Schools. The program featured the *Ruy Blas* Overture and Piano Concerto in G minor, Op.25 by Mendelssohn, and an inspirational cantata, *The Golden Legend* by Sir Arthur Sullivan.

Just four days later, the first Young People's Concert was held, featuring the music of Sousa, Dvořák, Schumann, Kreisler, Grainger and Johann Strauss Jr., including a performance of Saint-Saëns' *Rondo Capriccioso* with violin soloist Walter Hagen. A seasonal medley of Christmas carols was included for good measure.

BPO educational programs have matured in tempo and tone with the growth of the Philharmonic itself. During the Valdes years, the Orchestra dramatically increased its educational outreach. As many as 125 Youth Concerts were offered in area schools, and more than 70 programs were offered at the University at Buffalo, Canisius College and SUNY Fredonia.

Education programs also expanded to include

David Mack, 10, leaves his front row seat to take a closer look during a 1961 concert in Kleinhans.

Buffalo school children attending a concert at Kleinhans during the 1949-50 season.

EVERYBODY LIKES MUSIC

Music-minded Erie County, now one of the nation's leading cultural centers, sent 140,000 of its residents to Kleinhans Music Hall during the past season to hear concerts played by the Buffalo Philharmonic Orchestra. The 1948-1949 figures include 30,000 persons who attended the 10 concerts of the symphony series; 40,000 who attended the 20 Friday night Pops Concerts; 40,000 school children who attended seven concerts for the city's public, private and parochial schools and four concerts for suburban schools; and 30,000 persons who attended the 1948 Summer concert series. It all goes to prove, according to Frank N. Farrar, president of the Buffalo Philharmonic Orchestra Society, that Longfellow was right and "music is the universal language of mankind." Everyone likes music if he has a chance to hear it at its best, Mr. Farrar believes, and—he points out—there are enough musical forms to satisfy every human taste. The aim of the Buffalo Philharmonic Orchestra, the president declares, is to provide the very best music in each of the various forms. These include music of the so-called "long-hair" type—the great symphonies, concerts and operas; the semi-classical, the modern classical, and the form represented by composers of popular airs beloved by American youth. All of these forms have been presented by the Buffalo Philharmonic Orchestra in a wide variety of programs in Kleinhans Music Hall. They have attracted a wide variety of audiences representing every neighborhood in the community. The photos on this page are typical of three audience groups regularly attending Philharmonic concerts. *Photos by Elizabeth Kahler*

COURIER EXPRESS, MARCH 20, 1949

CHILDREN en route up the broad stairway of Kleinhans Music Hall at a Wednesday afternoon concert welcome the opportunity to be photographed.

(Left) MUSIC of the Buffalo Philharmonic Orchestra holds the young audience in its spell

A school bus drops students off at Kleinhans in the late 1950s.

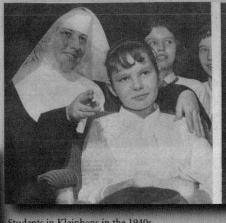

Students in Kleinhans in the 1940s.

School children singing during an Akron Community Night in 2010. Sue Fay Allen in the foreground, founded Community Nights.

Harpist Suzanne Thomas shows school children her beautiful instrument during the 1975-76 season.

A BPO performance at North Tonawanda High School on May 28, 1970 conducted by John Landis.

Preparing Orchestra Syllabus for Schools

League of American Orchestras Conducting Fellow Joseph Young leads a rehearsal for an education concert.

Mrs. Robert Dobie and BPO manager Robert MacIntyre working on an innovative school syllabus in September 1950 to help teachers prepare students for concerts. This is still done today.

Paul Ferrington conducts an education concert on June 30, 2007.

JoAnn Falletta teaches performance technique during the BRAVO International Chamber Music Workshop to the Vivace-Adagio-Allegro group in Dunleavy Amphitheater at Niagara University.

JoAnn Falletta with Yo-Yo Ma.

PHOTOGRAPH BY HARRY SCULL JR., THE BUFFALO NEWS

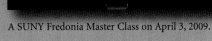

They're Not for Old Squares

Orchestra Notes to Spur Child Interest in Classics

By BOB LECKIE

It was not so long ago school children would sit on their hands and snap their bubble gum to relieve the ordeal of a classical music concert. But this Winter, chances are that in Buffalo they will be chasing their old dread of things classical with an eager curiosity to hear what old Johann Strauss wrote on his shirtcuff in Vienna that day.

Such a remarkable change in the traditional schoolboy attitude is likely to occur through the influence of a 74-page syllabus for teachers made public yesterday by Manager Robert E. MacIntyre of the Buffalo Philharmonic Orchestra.

The syllabus is a study of the Youth Concerts to be held in Kleinhans Music Hall by the Buffalo Philharmonic this year for school children in public, parochial and private schools of Buffalo and Western New York.

It is designed to supply the classroom teacher with program notes and other material which will prepare the student for the concerts.

No Longhair Stuff

Far from being longhair, the syllabus is as free from jargon as Mother Goose. Through its use in the class-

groups to numbers from the musicals, South Pacific.

In Buffalo, the program is for children in the sixth, seventh and eighth grades. Pupils will be required to attend one concert and listen to radio broadcasts of the remaining six.

The broadcasts, said MacIntyre, are made possible through a grant of funds from Mrs. William L. Marcy, made in memory of E. M. Statler, Buffalonian and founder of the Hotels Statler. For schools outside of Buffalo, the programs are for pupils in the sixth grade through high school.

One of Finest Projects

According to MacIntyre, the Buffalo Philharmonic's program of Youth Concerts is "one of the finest projects of its kind in the country."

"Our programs have been studied

A SUNY Fredonia Master Class on April 3, 2009.

BUFFALO PHILHARMONIC ORCHESTRA
BPO
Key into Music
LEARNING RESOURCE GUIDE FOR GRADES K-6 PEOPLE OF HOMES

Community Spotlight, a collaboration between the Buffalo Philharmonic and the Erie County Music Educators Association (ECMEA) was initially conceived in 1994 by Sue Fay Allen, former Music Coordinator for the Amherst Schools. Students perform in the Mary Seaton Room prior to BPO Classics concerts. Public, private and community orchestras, bands, choruses and ensembles of every variety participate, with seating for a large audience around tables. Participants receive complimentary tickets for the evening's BPO concert. For participating students, the chance to perform for a pre-concert audience at a BPO concert in Kleinhans is exciting in itself.

To honor Western New York music educators, the BPO hosts the Celebration of Music Education event each year in partnership with BOCES. Exceptional music educators are recognized through annual Awards for Excellence in Music Education. Friends of the BPO also awards Young Persons' Scholarships to musically-talented high school seniors. All awards are presented during a BPO classics concert in Kleinhans.

At the university level, hundreds of on-campus concerts take place, featuring programming from the Baroque Age through the avant-garde. The BPO has performed often with the Fredonia College Choir, including tour appearances at Lincoln Center. The Orchestra has also performed at new music concerts at Cornell, and at UB's North American New Music Festival and June in Buffalo, and on tour across New York State at nearly all campuses in the SUNY system. Some BPO musicians also serve on the faculty of these schools.

BPO ARCHIVES

BUFFALO PHILHARMONIC ORCHESTRA
60TH ANNIVERSARY SEASON
1995 - 1996

MAXIMIANO VALDES, MUSIC DIRECTOR
DOC SEVERINSEN, PRINCIPAL POPS CONDUCTOR

The New
Buffalo
Philharmonic
Orchestra
'94-'95

MAXIMIANO VALDES, MUSIC DIRECTOR
DOC SEVERINSEN, PRINCIPAL POPS CONDUCTOR

The 60th Anniversary season program in 1995-96 is festive. The 1994-95 season program features Valdes and Doc Severinsen – the "New" BPO.

Sonata for Sitting Ducks

TOM TOLLES, IN *THE BUFFALO NEWS*, NOVEMBER 11, 1990 AND SEPTEMBER 30, 1993

Political cartoonist Tom Tolles riffs off the BPO's financial woes in November 1990 and September 1993.

THE BUFFALO NEWS, JUNE 28, 1994 AND THE BUFFALO NEWS, JUNE 30, 1994

Orchestra officials voice optimism
Philharmonic agreement guarantees music for at least 3 years

Musicians OK orchestra pact
Summer schedule canceled; members take 5% pay cut, lower health benefits

Contract negations in 1994 resulted in the BPO musicians accepting a 5 percent pay cut. These were difficult times.

continued from page 97

and at Artpark. Miller delighted audiences with his televised "Sing Along with Mitch" style from the 1960s. He also turned out exciting performances of Rossini overtures, Strauss waltzes and a variety of showcase works like Ravel's *Bolero*.

With his silver "Tonight Show" trumpet in hand, Doc Severinsen took over the Pops podium in Kleinhans Music Hall in 1992. Through eight straight seasons, Severinsen's many sold-out concerts featured leading pop, jazz and Broadway soloists in top-of-the-line Hollywood arrangements, in addition to his wailing solos on lead trumpet. On October 22, 1994, under the baton of Valdes, Severinsen was also the featured soloist in the world premiere of *American Concerto for Trumpet* by Ellen Zwilich.

"THE CROWD THAT TURNED OUT FOR THE EVENT [ARENA MAGIC...CATCH IT!] WAS TREATED TO TV PERSONALITIES, NATIVE AMERICAN DANCERS, ICE SKATERS, ATHLETES, POLITICIANS AND A HEALTHY DOSE OF BUFFALO HISTORY AND PRIDE."

– *THE BUFFALO NEWS*
SEPTEMBER 28, 1996

Under Miller and Severinsen, both the standard Pops as well as "Beer & Jeans" concerts featured well-known film, stage and jazz personalities including Peter Nero, Canadian Brass, P.D.Q. Bach (Peter Schickele), Skitch Henderson, Danny Kaye and Henri Mancini, among many others.

During Valdes' tenure, WNED-FM taped and broadcast several BPO concerts, including the live performance on October 25, 1987 of Mozart's Symphony No.36 *"Linz."*

The BPO has a long history of performing at the dedications of important local venues, including Kleinhans Music Hall and Artpark. Right on cue, for the gala opening of the Marine Midland Arena on September 27, 1996, the BPO was featured with local and national star Ani DiFranco under the direction of Pops maestro Doc Severinsen – a sort of modern "Monster Pop Concert." The program was billed as "Arena Magic...Catch it!"

CHAPTER 11

THE FALLETTA YEARS

1998-

JOANN FALLETTA

BORN
February 27, 1954
Queens, New York City, New York

STUDIED
Classical guitar, conducting

CURRENTLY
Longest serving Music Director
in the BPO's history

FIRST BPO CONCERT
At Artpark - July 17, 1993 (guest conductor)
Berlioz - *Roman Carnival Overture*
Rossini - *Introduction Theme and Variations
for Clarinet and Orchestra*
Orff - *Carmina Burana*
    John Fullam, clarinet soloist

BUFFALO HIGHLIGHTS
- Two Grammy Awards with BPO,
  including "Best Performance"
- 18 CDs, including 10 on Naxos label
- Established the *JoAnn Falletta International
  Guitar Concerto Competition*
- Named to Buffalo's Music Hall
  of Fame in 2010
- National broadcasts of NPR's
  Performance Today, From The Top
  and *SymphonyCast*
- International broadcasts through the
  European Broadcasting Union
- Brought the BPO back to
  Carnegie Hall after 25 years
- Received the Foundation for Jewish
  Philanthropies Award for the Marcel
  Tyberg Musical Legacy project
- March 2010 "Florida Friends Tour"

PHOTOGRAPH BY MARK DELLAS

CAREER HIGHLIGHTS
- First woman to lead a major
  U.S. symphony orchestra
- Won the coveted Stokowski Competition,
  and received the Toscanini, Ditson, Bruno
  Walter, John S. Edwards and Seaver/
  NEA Awards for conducting
- Presidential appointee to the National
  Council on the Arts, 2009
- Hailed as a "leading force for the music
  of our time," ASCAP has honored her
  with 10 awards
- Music Director, Virginia Symphony
- Music Director, Long Beach
  Symphony Orchestra

"We celebrate 75 years of great music, as well as the hundreds of extremely talented musicians who have made up the Buffalo Philharmonic, the illustrious guest artists and conductors who have graced our stage, the composers whose works have soared into sonic life in this hall. But most of all, we celebrate the countless members of our audience, the patrons and donors and sponsors who have supported and cherished our BPO, the community which has embraced us and kept our music vibrant and thriving in good times and in challenging ones as well."

- JOANN FALLETTA

CHAPTER 11
THE FALLETTA YEARS
1998-

BPO MUSICIANS 2010-2011

FIRST VIOLIN
Michael Ludwig, Concertmaster
Amy Glidden
Ansgarius Aylward
Marylouise Nanna
Douglas Cone
Frances Kaye
Karen Soffer
Deborah Greitzer
Diana Sachs
Alan Ross
Melanie Haas
Andrea Blanchard-Cone
Loren Silvertrust

SECOND VIOLIN
Antoine Lefebvre
Jacqueline Galluzzo
Richard Kay
Jeffrey Jones
Frances Morgante
Donald McCrorey
Robert Prokes

Amy Licata
Dmitry Gerikh
Diane Melillo
Shieh-Jian Tsai

VIOLA
Valerie Heywood
Natalie Piskorsky
Marcia Bettigole
Matthew Phillips
Kate Holzemer
Janz Castelo
Ning-ning Jin

CELLO
Roman Mekinulov
Feng Hew
Nancy Anderson
Monte Hoffman
Robert Hausmann
David Schmude
Amelie Fradette

BASS
Daniel Pendley
Brett Shurtliffe
William Burns
Michael Nigrin
John Haas
Makoto Michii
Edmond Gnekow

FLUTE
Christine Lynn Bailey
Betsy Reeds
Natalie Debikey-Scanio

PICCOLO
Natalie Debikey-Scanio

OBOE
Catherine Estes
Anna Mattix

ENGLISH HORN
Anna Mattix

CLARINET
John Fullam
Patti Dilutis
Salvatore Andolina

E-FLAT CLARINET
Patti Dilutis

**BASS CLARINET &
SAXOPHONE**
Salvatore Andolina

BASSOON
Glenn Einschlag
Ron Daniels
Martha Malkiewicz

CONTRABASSOON
Martha Malkiewicz

FRENCH HORN
Jacek Muzyk
Daniel Kerdelewicz
Daniel Sweeley
Jay Matthews
Duane Saetveit

TRUMPET
Alex Jokipii
Geoffrey Hardcastle
Philip Christner

TROMBONE
Jonathan Lombardo
Timothy Smith

BASS TROMBONE
Jeffrey Dee

TUBA
Don Harry

TIMPANI
Matthew Bassett
Dinesh Joseph

PERCUSSION
Mark Hodges
Dinesh Joseph

HARP
Suzanne Thomas

**BUFFALO
PHILHARMONIC
CHORUS**
Doreen Rao, Music Director

NOTABLE GUEST CONDUCTORS

Philippe Entremont, pianist, conductor | January 27, 2001
Michael Tilson Thomas, conductor | March 17, 2001
Jaime Laredo, conductor | April 21 & 22, 2001
Sergiu Comissiona, conductor | May 19 & 20, 2001
Kenneth Schermerhorn, guest conductor |
   November 17 & 18, 2001
Ronald Zollman, conductor | February 15 & 16, 2002
Yoav Talmi, conductor | March 1 & 2, 2002
Julius Rudel, conductor | April 13 & 14, 2002
Pinchas Zukerman, violinist, conductor |
   January 31 & February 1, 2003
Lukas Foss, guest conductor | April 12 & 13, 2003
Eiji Oue, guest conductor | April 26 & 27, 2003

Jahja Ling, conductor | May 31 & June 1, 2003
James Judd, conductor | November 1 & 2, 2003
Maximiano Valdes, conductor | November 22 & 23, 2003
Arthur Fagen, conductor | December 5 & 6, 2003
Jorge Mester, conductor | February 20 & 21, 2004
Fabio Mechetti, conductor | October 30 & 31, 2004
Andrew Litton, conductor | January 22 & 23, 2005
Daniel Hege, conductor | March 4 & 5, 2005
Keith Lockhart, conductor | November 5 & 6, 2005
Roberto Minczuk, conductor | January 28 & 29, 2006
Gian Carlo Guerrero, conductor | April 22 & 23, 2006
Gerard Schwarz, conductor | March 31 & April 1, 2007

Ignat Solzhenitsyn, conductor and pianist | May 12 & 13, 2007
Michael Morgan, conductor | February 16 & 17, 2008
Zuohuang Chen, conductor | April 25 & 26, 2008
Maximiano Valdes, conductor | November 15 & 16, 2008
Andreas Delfs, conductor | January 24 & 25, 2009
Alvaro Cassuto, conductor | March 21 & 22, 2009
Bruno Ferrandis, conductor | May 2 & 3, 2009
Michael Christie, guest conductor | November 21 & 22, 2009
Bernhard Gueller, guest conductor | December 4 & 5, 2009
Jorge Mester, guest conductor | February 5, & 6, 2010
Christopher Wilkins, guest conductor | March 27 & 28, 2010
Marvin Hamlisch, guest conductor | April 24, 2010

NOTABLE GUEST SOLOISTS

Benita Valente, soprano | February 7 & 8, 1998
Arturo Sandoval, trumpeter | September 18, 1999
André-Michel Schub, pianist | October 1 & 2, 1999
Tomohiro Okumura, violinist | October 23 & 24, 1999
Yo-Yo Ma, cellist | December 3, 1999
Horacio Gutiérrez, pianist | March 4 & 5, 2000
Charles Haupt, violinist | April 1 & 2, 2000
John Browning, pianist | May 6 & 7, 2000
Lara St. John, violinist | May 19 & 20, 2000
Kaori Sato, soprano | September 23 & 24, 2000
Raul Melo, tenor | September 23 & 24, 2000
Louis Lortie, pianist | October 21, 2000
Nadia Salerno-Sonnenberg, violinist | November 18 & 19, 2000
Anthony Newman, harpsichordist | December 16 & 17, 2000
Santiago Rodriguez, pianist | January 12 & 13, 2001
Pamela Frank, violinist | February 2 & 3, 2001
Carter Brey, cellist | February 16 & 17, 2001
Angel Romero, guitarist | March 2, 3 & 4, 2001
Evelyn Glennie, percussionist | March 31 & April 1, 2001
Misha Dichter, pianist | May 5 & 6, 2001
Barbara Quintiliani, soprano | June 8 & 9, 2001
Van Cliburn, pianist | October 6, 2001
Richard Goode, pianist | October 13 & 14, 2001
Midori, violinist | October 27 & 28, 2001
Emanuel Ax, pianist | December 1 & 2, 2001
Carol Wincenc, flutist | January 18 & 19, 2002
Gary Graffmann, pianist | February 1 & 2, 2002
Claudine Carlson, mezzo-soprano | June 8 & 9, 2002
Renée Fleming, soprano | September 21, 2002
Eroica Trio | October 19 & 20, 2002
David Shifrin, clarinetist | November 2 & 3, 2002

Robert McDuffie, violinist | March 7 & 8, 2003
Sharon Isbin, guitarist | April 4 & 5, 2003
Jon Nakamatsu, pianist | April 12 & 13, 2003
Cecile Licad, pianist | May 10 & 11, 2003
Adele Anthony, violinist | May 31 & June 1, 2003
Itzhak Perlman, violinist | June 21, 2003
Nadja Salerno-Sonnenberg, violinist | September 20, 2003
Regina Carter, jazz violinist | September 20, 2003
Eileen Ivers, fiddler-violinist | September 20, 2003
Ilya Gringolts, violinist | October 18 & 19, 2003
Elmar Oliveira, violinist | November 22 & 23, 2003
William VerMeulen, French hornist | December 5 & 6, 2003
Roman Mekinulov, cellist | January 3 & 4, 2004
Sebnem Mekinulov, soprano | April 17 & 18, 2004
Joshua Bell, violinist | May 1 & 2, 2004
Norman Krieger, pianist | October 16 & 17, 2004
Dawn Upshaw, soprano | February 18 & 19, 2005
Yura Lee, violinist | March 18 & 19, 2005
Gil Shaham, violinist | April 16, 2005
Cho-Liang Lin, violinist | June 4 & 5, 2005
Jean Louis Steuerman, pianist | October 1 & 2, 2005
Orli Shaham, piano | November 5 & 6, 2005
Renee Fleming, soprano | February 18, 2006
Paul Neubauer, viola | March 4 & 5, 2006
William Wolfram, pianist | March 18 & 19, 2006
Ian Parker, pianist | April 22 & 23, 2006
William Eddins, pianist | May 6 & 7, 2006
Daniel Binelli, bandoneon | June 3 & 4, 2006
Sarah Chang, violinist | September 16, 2006
Benedetto Lupo, pianist | September 30 & October 1, 2006
Hila Plitmann, soprano | March 3 & 4, 2007

Stefan Jackiw, violinist | March 16 & 17, 2007
Michael Ludwig, violinist | April 13 & 14, 2007
Van Cliburn, pianist | September 15, 2007
Philippe Bianconi, pianist | September 29 & 30, 2007
Sa Chen, pianist | October 12 & 13, 2007
Joan Kwuon, violinist | January 26 & 27, 2008
Sir James Galway, flutist | February 23, 2008
Lady Jeanne Galway, flutist | February 23, 2008
Anna Polonsky, pianist | March 15 & 16, 2008
Edgar Meyer, contrabass | April 25 & 26, 2008
Igor Lipinski, pianist | May 10 & 11, 2008
Itzhak Perlman, violinist | September 27, 2008
Enrica Ciccarelli, pianist | November 1 & 2, 2008
Anne-Marie McDermott, pianist | November 29, 2008
André Watts, pianist | February 21, 2009
Robert McDuffie, violinist | March 21 & 22, 2009
Muza Rubackyte, pianist | April 4 & 5, 2009
Elizabeth Hogue, soprano | April 17 & 18, 2009
Norman Krieger, pianist | May 2 & 3, 2009
Mary Wilson, soprano | June 13 & 14, 2009
Stacey Rishoi, mezzo-soprano | June 13 & 14, 2009
Johnny Mathis, vocalist | September 26, 2009
Adele Anthony, violinist | October 3, 2009
Ben Folds, pianist | October 8, 2009
Chris Botti, jazz trumpeter | October 24, 2009
Peter Serkin, pianist | February 20, 2010
Rita Moreno, singer | February 27, 2010
Fabio Bidini, pianist | March 6, 2010
Evelyn Glennie, percussionist | April 17 & 18, 2010
Steve Lippia, vocalist | May 8, 2010

CHAIRMEN OF THE BPO BOARD OF DIRECTORS

1997-1999 Mr. Robert M. Greene
1999-2001 Mr. Thomas P. Hartnett, Ph.D.

2001-2004 Mr. James D. Newman
2004-2008 Mr. Angelo M. Fatta, Ph.D.

2008-2010 Ms. Cheryl Howe
2011- Ms. Cindy Abbott Letro

THE FALLETTA YEARS

1998-

The year 1998 was a one of science and serendipity. Astronomers searched and found that the universe would expand forever. Google launched its search engine. The City of Buffalo restored the magnificent sunburst skylight on the 13th floor of its City Hall, adding a flood of symbolic light over the Common Council Chambers. Eileen Collins became the first woman to command a NASA space shuttle. And JoAnn Falletta became the first woman to serve as the music director of a major symphony orchestra.

When JoAnn Falletta stepped to the podium in Kleinhans Music Hall, she was already a rising star in the music world. She had been appointed Music Director of the Virginia Symphony in 1991 – a position she still holds 20 years later – and had served as Music Director for the Long Beach Symphony, Denver Chamber Orchestra and Bay Area Women's Philharmonic, all in addition to acting as Artistic Advisor for the Honolulu Symphony.

While pursuing her undergraduate degree at the Mannes School of Music, Falletta decided to add a conducting major to her studies on classical guitar. Despite the initial reluctance of the Mannes administration to sanction a female conducting student, given their reservations about whether a woman would ever be appointed Music Director of a major symphony, they acquiesced. Falletta studied with Jorge Mester and earned her degree. Later, she would study as a Master of Arts student with a conductor who would precede her on the

JoAnn Falletta in Kleinhans Music Hall.

Kleinhans podium – Semyon Bychkov – and take several conducting classes with Leonard Bernstein before earning her Masters and Doctoral degrees in conducting from Juilliard.

Her first appearance with the Buffalo Philharmonic was at Artpark in the summer of 1993 when she conducted *Carmina Burana*. She first appeared with the Orchestra at Kleinhans for a performance of Handel's *Messiah* in December 1997. Just weeks prior to her appointment, on February 7, 1998 Falletta led the BPO in a splendid program that included the *Prelude* and *Liebestod* from Wagner's *Tristan and Isolde*, Mozart's *Exsultate, Jubilate* and Dvořák's *Hymn to the Moon* from *Rusalka*, featuring soprano Benita Valente. The concert concluded with Rachmaninoff's *Symphonic Dances*. The audience and the musicians alike filled the hall with bravos and hearty applause. Interviews with the Orchestra's board of directors followed, and after

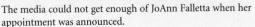

The media could not get enough of JoAnn Falletta when her appointment was announced.

Symphony Magazine published a feature article on the significance of the $6 million challenge grant received by the BPO in 2008 and the exceptional support of the Buffalo community that it represented.

a few schedule adjustments, voilà! The BPO had a new maestro, one who would remain on the podium longer than any of her predecessors.

Falletta's opening night was magnificent. On November 14, 1998, the rapt audience enjoyed Hindemith's *Symphonic Metamorphosis on Themes by Weber*, Mendelssohn's Piano Concerto No.1 in G minor, op. 25 and Tchaikovsky's Symphony No.5 in E minor, op. 64.

Falletta has proven to be an exceptionally versatile conductor. In addition to her mastery of the standard orchestral repertoire, she is ever on the look-out for new and intriguing scores from around the world, very much in sync with the multi-national nature of the BPO. Classics programs are typically diverse, with a host of celebrated soloists – the velvet poetry of Itzhak Perlman, the fireworks

"MS. FALLETTA IS A DEMONSTRATIVE, KINETIC CONDUCTOR, AND HER GESTURES… ACHIEVED CLEAR RESULTS. IN PARTICULAR, SHE BROUGHT A LOVELY SWEEP TO THE ELGAR, *ENIGMA* VARIATIONS, AND ELICITED NOT ONLY A WARM STRING SOUND BUT ALSO SUPERBLY DETAILED WIND AND BRASS PLAYING."

- THE NEW YORK TIMES

of Nadia Salerno-Sonnenberg, the grace and charm of Van Cliburn, the uplifting joy of Yo-Yo Ma and amber arias of Renée Fleming – performing a variety of music both familiar and new.

Under Falletta, the Orchestra returned to touring, has regained its position as a recording ensemble, and has improved the always-perilous financial situation through the completion of a $30 million endowment campaign to "Secure The Future" in 2008.

The expansion of the BPO's endowment through a five-year campaign remains one of the signature non-artistic achievements of Falletta's tenure. Orchestras typically seek to have an endowment which is at least triple their annual operating budget, to allow them to offset potential losses and budget for a fairly stable income source. While the BPO had

VAN CLIBURN

PHOTO BY PHIL KLEM

PHOTO BY DINESH JOSEPH

PHOTO BY DINESH JOSEPH

Celebrating the BPO's
75th Anniversary
The Florida Friends Tour
March 2010

Falletta led the BPO on its first tour in more than 25 years in March 2010.
The five-city tour was an enormous success, both artistically and financially.

BPO ARCHIVES

long enjoyed enough community support to continue as a going concern, the frequent lurches in financial fortunes strained musicians, staff and supporters.

Taking the reins of an endowment campaign in 2003, Board Chairman Dr. Angelo M. Fatta joined with Executive Director Daniel Hart and Falletta to "Secure the Future." Over the course of five years, the campaign raised $32 million in pledges and contributions, closing out with a matching grant that put them "over the top" at the end of 2008. While the subsequent turbulence of the financial markets has seen this number ebb and flow, the endowment will play a major role in ensuring that the BPO's rich legacy in Western New York continues for years to come.

Touring has long been acknowledged as an important part of any ensemble's artistic development, and the BPO experienced this for the first time since the 1985 European Tour when Falletta led the ensemble on tour in March 2010. Resuming its position as Buffalo's cultural ambassador, "The Florida Friends Tour" included concerts in Fort Lauderdale, Daytona Beach, Vero Beach, Sarasota and Gainesville. It was a thrill for the many Buffalo expatriates and snowbirds wintering in Florida to attend these concerts with pride, and there were many hugs and handshakes backstage in every city. They made the tour both an artistic and financial success, enabling the BPO to post a balanced budget during the financial stress of the 2009-10 season.

continued on page 111

Van Cliburn has practically become part of the BPO extended family during his numerous appearances with the BPO over the past 54 years, despite a few mishaps. Prior to his most recent performance of Tchaikovsky's Piano Concerto No.1 with the Philharmonic in September 2007, the pianist recalled his first BPO appearance in Kleinhans with Josef Krips on March 13, 1956, when the pedals fell off the piano during a performance of Schumann's Piano Concerto in A minor. The concert was stopped. Unfortunately the piano technician had already left the Hall. The day was saved when a clarinet player managed to reattach the pedals and the concerto was restarted.

By bizarre coincidence, during another Van Cliburn appearance, this time at Artpark in August 1994, the lid of the Steinway grand crashed to the floor of the stage, narrowly missing the toes of the first stand of violas.

Despite these stage glitches, Van Cliburn had warm praise for the BPO and expressed how much he likes the superb acoustics of Kleinhans Music Hall.

GRAMMY AWARDS AND GLOBAL ACCLAIM

Recordings and broadcasts and have long been the mark of artistic excellence in the world of classical music. Like orchestra tours, they send an instant message about an orchestra's performance level and the depth of its players. They also bring the sound of music made in Buffalo to the world.

Since the first recording in 1946 of Shostakovich's Symphony No.7 *"Leningrad"* under William Steinberg's baton, more than 44 recordings have been made by the BPO.

BPO WINS TWO GRAMMY AWARDS

This illustrious history of recording culminated in 2009, when the release of John Corigliano's *Mr. Tambourine Man: Seven Poems of Bob Dylan* won not one, but two Grammy Awards: one for Best Classical Performance and the other for Best Classical Contemporary Composition. This is an extraordinary honor for a philharmonic orchestra.

Following the appointment of Falletta as music director in 1998, changes in the musician's master contract (EMG, Electronic Media Guarantee) paved the way to a robust renewal of BPO broadcasts and recordings. As of 2010, no fewer than 20 new CDs have been released during the Falletta years alone. Eight are on the Naxos label, featuring the music of Respighi, Richard Strauss and Schubert, and five were released by Naxos as part of its American Classics

Concertmaster Michael Ludwig, composer John Corigliano and JoAnn Falletta discuss the score before a recording session.

PHOTOGRAPH BY ENID BLOCH

Soprano Hila Plitmann (*below*) performs on the Grammy Award-winning *Mr. Tambourine Man* recording under the baton of Falletta.

PHOTOGRAPH BY MARC ROYCE

BPO ARCHIVES

PHOTOGRAPH FROM WVPUBCASTORE

A fine distinction for the BPO came in 2009 when its recording of Corigliano's *Mr. Tambourine Man: Seven Poems of Bob Dylan* won two Grammy Awards, one for Best Classical Performance and the other for Best Classical Contemporary Composition.

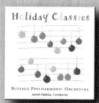

Church Windows, Brazilian Impressions, Rossiniana (2007, Naxos) received a nomination for Best Engineered Album, Classical for work by recording engineer John Newton.

RESPIGHI
Church Windows
Brazilian Impressions
Rossiniana
Buffalo Philharmonic Orchestra
JoAnn Falletta

AMERICAN CLASSICS
CHARLES GRIFFES
The Pleasure Dome of Kubla Khan
The White Peacock · Three Poems of Fiona McLeod

Barbara Quintiliani, Soprano · Carol Wincenc, Flute
Buffalo Philharmonic Orchestra · JoAnn Falletta

SCHUBERT
Death and the Maiden
(String Quartet in D minor adapted by Andy Stein)
Symphony No. 8, 'Unfinished'
(Completed by Brian Newbould and Mario Venzago)
Buffalo Philharmonic Orchestra · JoAnn Falletta

Richard
STRAUSS
Josephs-Legende · Rosenkavalier
Die Frau ohne Schatten
(Orchestral Suites)
Buffalo Philharmonic Orchestra · JoAnn Falletta

Blanton Alspaugh was nominated as Producer of the Year, Classical for his body of work that includes the BPO recording, *Schubert: Death and the Maiden* (2008, Naxos)

Beautiful music in the morning!
WNED program host Scott Sackett and BPO music director JoAnn Falletta introduce recent BPO performances recorded in concert.

PHILHARMONIC FRIDAY
Fridays at 10 am

Classical
94.5 / WNED
Classical music - All day and all night
wned.org/fm

AMERICAN CLASSICS
AARON COPLAND
Rodeo
(Four Dance Episodes)
The Red Pony (Suite)
Prairie Journal
Letter from Home
Buffalo Philharmonic Orchestra
JoAnn Falletta

AMERICAN OPERA CLASSICS
Daron HAGEN
Shining Brow
Libretto by Paul Muldoon
Orth · Harris · Frankenberry · Curran · Valby · Lyons
Buffalo Philharmonic Orchestra and Chorus
JoAnn Falletta

Marcel TYBERG
(1893-1944)
Symphony No. 3
Piano Trio
Michael Ludwig, Violin
Roman Mekinulo, Cello
Ya-Fei Chuang, Piano
Buffalo Philharmonic Orchestra
JoAnn Falletta

Impressions of French Music

Buffalo Philharmonic Orchestra at Carnegie Hall
JoAnn Falletta, Conductor

---

series featuring the music of John Corigliano, Aaron Copland, Charles Griffes, William Converse and Daron Hagen.

Under Falletta's direction the Orchestra also issued two Holiday CDs, followed by a third titled "Holiday Pops," conducted by Marvin Hamlisch. In 2007, the Buffalo Philharmonic Chorus released a CD with the BPO of *Passage Into Spirit* by Randol Alan Bass.

ON THE AIR
The BPO was heard over the airwaves even before it was first recorded. Regular WBEN radio broadcasts date back to the mid-1930s and a valuable partnership with WNED has led to many broadcasts over the years. The BPO has been consistently featured on national broadcasts of NPR's "Performance Today" and "SymphonyCast." The BPO is the only major orchestra to be featured twice on NPR's "From the Top." Other recent broadcasts include a national PBS televised special, Bernstein's *"Ode to Freedom"* featuring Falletta as host, and a PBS special of the *Four Seasons* with Mark O'Connor and Catherine Cho. The BPO has also been heard abroad through the European Broadcasting Union.

The BPO has been one of Buffalo's best cultural ambassadors over the past 75 years.

Christopher O'Riley, pianist and host of NPR's "From the Top," performed with the BPO in March 2011. The concert, conducted by Falletta, aired the week of August 16.

Violinist and composer Mark O'Connor performed his own composition with the BPO in Kleinhans for the PBS television special "American Seasons," which aired on January 1, 2008.

MARCEL TYBERG

Marcel Tyberg was born in Vienna on Mozart's birthday in 1893 and fled with his family from the crumbling Austrian Empire for the Italian-controlled Adriatic Coast following World War I. With the collapse of the dictatorship of Benito Mussolini in 1943, Nazi persecution and detention of those with Jewish relations increased. Tyberg was one-sixteenth Jewish and a practicing Catholic.

After entrusting manuscripts of his compositions to Dr. Milan Mihich, a friend of the Tyberg family, Tyberg was picked up by the Gestapo in September, 1943. He died at Auschwitz on New Year's Eve, 1944.

The elder Mihich fled the Dalmatian coast as Communist Yugoslavs took over, arriving in Milan. Upon his death, in 1948, custody of the Tyberg documents fell to his son, Dr. Enrico (Henry) Mihich, who came to Buffalo to work at Roswell Park Cancer Institute in 1957. Mihich tried for decades to focus attention on the forgotten composer. Finally, in 2005, he found a partner in JoAnn Falletta.

Falletta's appreciation for Tyberg's artistry led to the painstaking reassembly of the manuscripts. Tyberg's Symphony No.3, the final work he composed, was performed by the BPO and released on the Naxos label in August 2010. In the spring of 2011, the BPO plans to perform the Second Symphony.

Of Polish lineage, Marcel Tyberg, (pronounced "TEE-berg") was born in Vienna on January 27, 1893. His father Marcell was a prominent violinist and his mother Wanda Paltinger Tybergova was a noted pianist and a colleague of Artur Schnabel in the renowned Leschetizky school of pianism.

Marcel Tyberg

Marcel TYBERG
(1893-1944)
Symphony No. 3
Piano Trio

Michael Ludwig, Violin
Roman Mekinulov, Cello
Ya-Fei Chuang, Piano

Buffalo Philharmonic Orchestra
JoAnn Falletta

In 1916, in the middle of World War I, the Tyberg family escaped the disintegrating Austrian Empire by moving to Abbazia, in the Northern Adriatic region of Italy.

Tyberg manuscript

Milan & Rosina Mihich

Shortly after completing his Third Symphony, with the Gestapo and the specter of death looking over his shoulder, Tyberg entrusted his manuscripts to long-time family friend, Dr. Milan Mihich, an Italian physician and music lover whose wartime home was near Abbazia.

Enrico (Henry) Mihich brought with him the Tyberg archives from Italy to Buffalo when he came to work at Roswell Park Cancer Institute in 1957. That is how the Tyberg archives migrated from Italy to Buffalo.

continued from page 107

From the first CD release of *Holiday Classics* by the BPO under Falletta in 1999, the Orchestra has released more than 20 recordings which have been distributed through both the BPO's signature imprint, Beau Fleuve, and received international distribution in partnership with NAXOS. Featuring a diverse repertoire from the Baroque to our modern era, the recordings offer an "on-the-record" self-portrait of the BPO at its artistic best.

Recordings have also enriched the BPO's collaboration with area cultural organizations.

IN TIMES OF ECONOMIC DIFFICULTY, THE ARTS, RATHER THAN LANGUISHING AS A DISCRETIONARY LUXURY, BECOMES MORE VITAL TO THE HUMAN CONDITION. THROUGH THE ARTS, WE HONOR OUR PAST, CELEBRATE OUR PRESENT AND DREAM OUR FUTURE. THE VERY BEST OF WHO WE ARE IS INHERENT IN THE ARTS, AND THE ARTS ARE AT THE CORE OF THE CONTINUAL REINVIGORATION OF OUR HUMANITY.

- JOANN FALLETTA, 2010

Paintings in the Albright-Knox Art Gallery inspired the *Pictures at a Gallery* recording in 2003, and Charles Burchfield's works at the Burchfield Penny Art Center underlie the *Tribute to Charles Burchfield* recording in 2004. In 2006, the BPO released Daron Hagen's *Shining Brow*, an opera based on the life of Frank Lloyd Wright. This continued a relationship with the architect's legacy which began in 2005 with a tribute to *Prairie Music*, which paired the music of Aaron Copland with Wright's prairie-style masterpiece, the Darwin Martin House.

When a concert begins, a conductor usually has a joyful task: to share great music with musicians and listeners alike. But there are times when a concert is solemn and sorrowful. This occurred during the Classics concert on September 15, 2001, following the tragic events of September 11. JoAnn Falletta opened the concert with solemn reverence, performing Elgar's *Nimrod* from the *Enigma Variations*. The collective grief and consolation was so moving, so inspirational that it created a bond that still resonates. At that moment, the audience and orchestra shared a single heart, a single soul – Kleinhans became a shrine in memoriam.

More than that, it became a moment of majesty. Three thousand people – a full house, the musicians, BPO staff, Kleinhans staff, volunteer ushers – made the decision to attend this particular concert because it was important – even essential – to be close to people of like mind and spirit.

PHOTOGRAPH COURTESY RON DANIELS

"It's quite remarkable to me that the tenures of conductors from Lajos Shuk to JoAnn Falletta have always seemed to be a perfect fit within Buffalo's history, and it seems obvious throughout these pages.

Maestro Falletta brings a singular ability to offer high artistic direction to us as musicians. But beyond that, she is an articulate, approachable highly regarded advocate for the Philharmonic throughout Western New York and beyond as we produce recordings, and broadcasts in unprecedented numbers - and even tour once again. Her tenure has been the longest, and I remain grateful for her abiding ambition that continues to guide us into the future."

- RON DANIELS
PRESIDENT, MUSICIANS LOCAL 92 AFM, 2010

ALL PHOTOGRAPHS BPO ARCHIVES

Dozens of notable guest soloists have graced the stage at Kleinhans during JoAnn Falletta's tenure. Pictured (*left to right*) are violinist Joan Kwuon, soprano Renée Fleming, violinist Gil Shaham, singer Sylvia McNair and singer Bernadette Peters.

VIOLINIST NADJA SALERNO-SONNENBERG PLAYED A LYRICAL AND HIGHLY ANIMATED INTERPRETATION OF BACH WITH THE BPO IN NOVEMBER, 2000. AFTER INTERMISSION SHE SLIPPED ON TO A SEAT IN THE BACK OF THE VIOLIN SECTION AND PLAYED AS IF SHE WERE A LONGTIME MEMBER OF THE ORCHESTRA, A DEMURE AND DEDICATED TEAM PLAYER IN TCHAIKOVSKY'S SYMPHONY NO.6.

In November 2009, the BPO joined with Neglia Ballet Artists for a new production of *The Nutcracker* conceived, designed and executed in Western New York, and presented in Buffalo's Art Deco masterpiece, Shea's Performing Arts Center. In 2010, the organization began a collaboration with the Buffalo & Erie County Public Library, bringing its "BPOvations" concert preview series to the Downtown, Orchard Park and Audubon branch libraries and also partnered in a revival of the Grosvenor Chamber Music Series.

The BPO's aggressive recording output has received acclaim from publications around the world and was recognized in 2009 with a pair of Grammy Awards for the recording of John Corigliano's *Mr. Tambourine Man: Six Songs of Bob Dylan* with soprano Hila Plitmann, for which the Orchestra was also given The Key to the City of Buffalo.

Diversity has been a hallmark of the BPO under Falletta. Not satisfied with simply re-reading the standard masterpieces, with which the Orchestra is equally at home, the recordings reflect the maestro's affinity for new and under-appreciated music. The rediscovery of the

ALL PHOTOGRAPHS BPO ARCHIVES

(*From left*) Violinist Robert McDuffie, pianist Igor Lipinski, pianist André Watts, violinist Midori and singer Rita Moreno.

BPO ARCHIVES

Cellist Yo-Yo Ma

PHOTOGRAPH BY AKIRO KINASHITA

Violinist Itzhak Perlman

music of Holocaust victim Marcel Tyberg and recordings of such early 20th Century composers as Charles Griffes and Frederick Converse illustrate this.

A recording also marked another artistic milestone for the BPO – the BPO's return in 2004 to Carnegie Hall after an absence of more than a decade and a half. Performing at Carnegie Hall is important, not only because it is the most prestigious concert venue in the U.S., equivalent in status to the Musikverein in Vienna, but also because of the Hall's splendid acoustics, the calibre of the New York audiences, and the respect accorded reviews in the City's newspapers and magazines. When the moment came for a return performance at Carnegie

under Falletta, it was a reaffirmation of the BPO as one of the great U.S. orchestras.

Performing works by Kodaly, Zemlinsky and Smetana, the June 6, 2004 performance by the BPO received rave reviews. The *Philadelphia Daily News* declared, "Falletta has inspired this Orchestra to an impressive level, blurring the category of the Big Five." The performance was also preserved on a 2005 Beau Fleuve release.

In keeping with the BPO's commitment to outreach and education, the first of the Carnegie Hall concerts on June 5, 2004 was part of the "Kidsnotes" series

continued on page 116

Many artists perform their scheduled concert with the BPO and while they are in town, also venture into the community. Violinist, composer, fiddler, Mark O'Connor taped a WNED special program, Dame Evelyn Glennie mingled with several hundred percussion students from Buffalo State and SUNY Colleges during a "Day of Percussion" which took place in the Mary Seaton Room, Spring 2010. Yo-Yo Ma spoke with students in an elementary school in September, 2005 and demonstrated his cello. He even allowed a young student to hold his bow while onlookers all held their collective breath.

JOANN FALLETTA INTERNATIONAL GUITAR CONCERTO COMPETITION

The inaugural *JoAnn Falletta International Guitar Concerto Competition* was a spectacular event that grabbed the attention of the guitar community around the globe. Organized by the BPO and WNED in 2004, the *Competition* was the first concerto competition for classical guitarists ever held. It is now considered one of the foremost guitar events in the world.

The semifinalists in 2004 hailed from Mexico, Germany, Uruguay, Argentina, Poland, Sweden, Brazil, Canada and the U.S. Marcin Dylla of Poland took First Place, capturing the title of first-ever winner of the *Competition*.

Joanne Castellani and Michael Andriaccio co-direct the *Competition* along with David Dusman. *Competition* contestants vie for prize packages that include cash, broadcast exposure, a concert guitar, and a concert tour, including a return engagement with the BPO and appearances with the Virginia Symphony, at the Round Top Music Festival in Texas and other venues. In a fun twist, the audience at the finals also selects the winner of the Audience Favorite Award,

Artist Hugo Rodriguez was named the official artist and his vibrant artwork graced the Competition's promotional materials, the Kleinhans stage and the Buffalo Niagara International Airport Art Gallery.

WNED and the Buffalo Philharmonic Orchestra present

The JoAnn Falletta International Guitar Concerto Competition

Artistic Directors, Joanne Castellani & Michael Andriaccio

June 9-13, 2008
Kleinhans Music Hall
Buffalo, New York USA

La Gytara Gytana - Gypsy Woman Guitar Official image of the JoAnn Falletta International Guitar Concerto Competition.

June 5-10, 2006
Kleinhans Music Hall
Buffalo, New York USA

2006 Festival program.

Joanne Castellani &
Michael Andriaccio,
co-artistic directors.

Kleinhans Music Hall with flags representing each country of 2010 competitors joined by the panel of judges and three winners.

The 2010 Festival winners receive their awards from JoAnn Falletta. (*From left to right*) Thomas Viloteau of France (Third Place), Nemanja Ostoji of Serbia (Second Place) and Artyom Dervoed of Russia (First Place).

Second Place winner
2010 Nemanja Ostoji
performs with JoAnn
Falletta conducting.

Who's Who of Classical Guitar Over the course of six years and four *Competitions*, the quality of the judges who have participated along with Joanne Castellani, Michael Andriaccio and David Dusman, is simply breathtaking.

Miguel del Aquila free-lance composer

Jack Behrens composer

Ernesto Bitetti internationally known classical guitarist

Carlos Bonell Grammy-nominated guitarist

Jeff Cogan guitarist and program director of the Orange County Guitar Circle

Michael Colina Grammy Award-winning jazz composer

Ernesto Cordero Composer and guitarist

Marcin Dylla winner of the first competition

Eduardo Fernandez world-renowned guitarist

David Frost critically acclaimed producer

Brian Head president, Guitar Foundation of America

Bruce Holzman Florida State University associate professor of guitar

John Landis Classical 94.5/WNED-FM program host

David Leisner leading classical guitarist

Tony Morris host of radio program Classical Guitar Alive!

Enrique Muñoz Teruel Spanish guitar virtuoso

Laura Oltman recital & chamber music guitarist

Eduardo Pascual Diez international classical guitarist

Micaela Pittaluga founder of the Alessandria International Guitar Competition & president of the Pittaluga Competition

Roberto Sierra leading composer

and Orchestra members choose the recipient of the BPO Musicians Choice Award.

Guitarists representing Peru, Canada, Japan, Mexico, Italy, Uruguay and the U.S. competed in the second *Competition* in 2006.

There were several firsts in 2008. "Guitar Days" was added to the roster of events, sending the international contestants out into the community, and the event was broadcast live on WNED-FM and streamed via the WNED website. This allowed the competitors' fans, friends and family to listen to their performances live from Buffalo, NY.

After three magnificent performances with the full Buffalo Philharmonic Orchestra in 2008, Laura Klemke of Germany was honored by the orchestra with the Musicians Award and three-time semifinalist Marco Sartor representing Uruguay took the Audience Favorite Award and was named First Place winner of the *Competition*.

Nine top guitarists representing eight nations were chosen participate in the fourth biennial *Competition* on June 1-4, 2010. Artyom Dervoed of Russia captured First place and the Audience Favorite Award, Nemanja Ostoji of Serbia placed Second, and Thomas Viloteau of France took Third Place and received the Musicians Award.

The Guitar Festival, as it has come to be affectionately known locally, is an excellent ambassador. Broadcast to an estimated 10 million people around the world, it puts Buffalo on the global map and shares Western New York's myriad cultural treasures with the world. Bravo!

REACHING YOUNG EARS

In 2008, the BPO's Education Series received the **Leonard Bernstein Award for Educational Programming** from The American Society of Composers, Authors and Publishers (ASCAP). Education concerts were under the direction of conductor Robert Franz.

Youth Concerts Area K-12 schools bus their students to Kleinhans Music Hall for programs on Pan-American Exposition, Erie Canal, Industrial Age, the Science of Sound and others. One-third of the students reached hear the BPO in their community.

Symphony Scholars High School students receive in-depth information about classical music and the orchestra, attend BPO concerts, and meet with soloists and conductors.

Artists In the Schools BPO musicians present programs and lectures in local schools.

Side by Side Concerts The Greater Buffalo Youth Orchestra, the Buffalo Academy of Visual and Performing Arts, and the Muhammad School of Music join the BPO in a mentoring experience culminating in a performance in Kleinhans.

BPOvations An informative series of lectures featuring the composers and repertoire of the current season, by professor and conductor Paul Ferrington.

Celebration of Music Education Honors exceptional music educators in Western New York. Friends of the BPO also awards Young Persons' Scholarships to musically-talented high school seniors. Co-sponsored by BOCES, awards are presented during a BPO Classics concert at Kleinhans.

Young Composers Forum Aspiring composers hear their compositions performed for the first time by a major symphony orchestra. Feedback from the musicians, the conductor and guest composers is also provided.

Family Concert Series & the BPO Instrument Zoo Before family concerts, children head to the "Instrument Zoo" in the Mary Seaton Room to play on a real orchestra instrument, visit with featured soloists and BPO players, and enjoy an unforgettable, hands-on experience.

West Side Connection Buffalo Public Schools on the city's West Side participate in guest artist visits and a concert in Kleinhans celebrating neighborhood diversity.

Executive Director Daniel Hart

Robert Franz conducting an education concert.

2000-05 Pops Conductor Marvin Hamlisch

Poster for a BPO production of *The Music Man.*

Associate Conductor Matthew Kraemer

Buffalo Chamber Players

continued from page 113

called Orchestra Power. Education and Youth concerts have been an important part of the BPO's presence in Western New York since Lajos Shuk conducted the first concerts for Buffalo Public Schools in 1935.

As of the BPO's 75th anniversary, total student attendance at youth concerts in Kleinhans Music Hall is conservatively estimated to approach the two-million mark. Beyond the Kleinhans experience, the BPO has also performed hundreds of concerts in public and private school auditoriums. Overall, full orchestral programs have been performed in 119 schools throughout Western New York, bringing great music to at least 250,000 students in their own schools.

The geographical outreach of the BPO's in-school youth concerts extends from Olean in the Southern Tier to Lake Ontario in the northwestern counties of New York State.

In 2008, under the guidance of then-Associate Conductor Robert Franz, the BPO's Education Series received the Leonard Bernstein Award for Educational Programming from ASCAP.

While the Music Director is the artistic force behind any Orchestra, he or she rarely conducts every program an ensemble performs during a given season. Given the especially wide range of concert offerings by the BPO – Classics, Pops, Youth, Family – like most other orchestras, the

Your BPO performs
LED-ZEPPELIN

Randy Jackson, vocals & Brett Havens, conductor

Friday, May 7, 8PM

Kleinhans Music Hall

Tickets start at just $29!

885-5000 | bpo.org

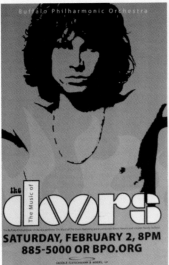

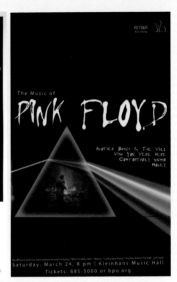

Frank Zappa actually hired the BPO in the 1980s to perform his orchestral works.

BPO must rely on a relay team of conductors, passing the baton from one venue or musical genre to the next.

Since 1998, the BPO Pops series has been offered under the batons of Principal Pops Conductors Doc Severinsen and Marvin Hamlisch, Associate Conductor Robert Franz, Ron Spigelman and current BPO Associate Conductor Matthew Kraemer.

As the long-term band leader of Johnny Carson's "Tonight Show," Severinsen has always traveled with his signature flash and panache. Among Doc's many memorable programs was his Valentine's Day concert on February 12, 1999, *Songs for Lovers and Others*. His mellow flugelhorn charmed the hearts of the sold-out Kleinhans crowd.

When Severinsen moved on after eight seasons with the BPO, he was succeeded by Marvin Hamlisch, who arrived on the Pops podium in the fall of 2000. Hamlisch's celebrity as a composer of Hollywood sound track music

and pop songs, as well as his droll wit and lyrical gift at the piano, provided many wonderful nights of music and laughter. In addition to his appearances at Holiday Pops, Hamlisch also arranged "tribute" concerts for artists such as Jerome Kern and Irving Berlin.

Such "tributes" have been expanded by the BPO in recent years to include Orchestral settings of popular rock groups like The Beatles, Led Zeppelin, Pink Floyd, The Doors and The Grateful Dead. Collaborations with singer-songwriters like Ben Folds and Buffalo's own Ani DiFranco, who opened the Marine Midland Arena (now HSBC arena) with Doc Severinsen, have expanded the BPO's presence and reach within the community.

After 75 Years, the BPO remains a vibrant and vital part of Western New York's cultural community with a dazzling array of concerts and programs which confirm that there truly is something for everybody at the BPO!

COMMUNITY SUPPORT

From its founding in 1935, the BPO has been sustained by a combination of ticket sales revenue, private contributions from patrons and local foundations, and by federal funding.

The Orchestra has been fortunate to receive generous support from the Greater Buffalo community, allowing it to survive many storms over the years. With continued support, the BPO will continue to make music for many years to come.

From the very first, the board of directors assumed full responsibility for the Orchestra's finances, including fundraising and accounting. Annual public appeals were made to keep the BPO's Maintenance Fund solvent for day-to-day operations, but always with a look to the future.

In September 2005, the BPO embarked on a $30 million endowment campaign dubbed "Secure the Future" meant to expand its endowment to match an industry standard of three times its $10 million operating budget.

Met with skepticism by some at the launch, the campaign surpassed the $30 million goal in just over three years, with 16 gifts in excess of $500,000, raising more than $32 million. While continued annual support remains critical, the endowment provides a solid foundation upon which the next 75 years and beyond can be built.

SECURE THE FUTURE

$30 million Endowment Campaign
2003-2008

$5,000,000+
The John R. Oishei Foundation

$2,000,000+
The Cameron and Jane Baird Foundation
Carol and Charles Balbach
Angelo and Carol Fatta
Peter and Elizabeth C. Tower
The Margaret L. Wendt Foundation

$1,000,000+
Elizabeth and John Angelbeck
Louis P. Ciminelli Family Foundation
The Garman Family Foundation
The Koessler Family
M&T Bank and Anonymous Friends
of the Bank

$500,000-999,999
Clement and Karen Arrison
Margaret W. Henry Trust
Mr. & Mrs. Robert Skerker
Jim and Michal Wadsworth as trustees of the
Mulroy, Heath and Colby Foundations

$250,000-499,999
The Baird Foundation
Benderson Family Foundation and
Delta Sonic Car Wash Systems
Anthony J. and Barbara Cassetta
Sally and Don Dussing
Inez Koop Estate
Carl and Carol Montante

$100,000-249,999
Gary and Willow Brost
The Buffalo News
Jerry and Barbara Castiglia
Anthony J. & Carmela M. Colucci
Community Foundation for Greater Buffalo
Charles and Nancy Dowdell
Neil and Doris Farmelo
Mr. & Mrs. John B. Fisher
Mr. and Mrs. Peter B. Flickinger
Ruth Geiger Estate
Gordon and Gretchen Gross
Grigg-Lewis Foundation
Mr. and Mrs. George G. Herbert
Bruce and Gail Johnstone
The Seymour H. Knox Foundation, Inc.
The Patrick P. Lee Foundation
Moog Inc.
Phyllis W. Pierce Charitable Lead Annuity Trust
Western New York Foundation
Wayne and Janet Wisbaum

$50,000-99,999
Cindy Abbott-Letro and Francis M. Letro
The Rev. and Mrs. Peter Bridgford
D-B Trust
Joseph Goodell* and Mary Ellen Hager
George S. Hoffman
Monte and Cheryl* Hoffman
John and Cheryl Howe
Hyde Family Charitable Fund
Jaeckle Fleischmann & Mugel, LLP
Linton/Kadet Family Foundation
Bob and Carolyn Montgomery

George and Carin Phillips
Mr. and Mrs. Edwin Polokoff
The Frank G. Raichle Foundation
Catherine F. Schweitzer
George G. and Elizabeth G. Smith Foundation
Harriet B. Stewart
James I. Stovroff Estate
Mrs. Robert Warner
Betty Ann Withrow

$25,000-49,999
Anonymous (2)
Mr.* and Mrs. William Christie
Nan and Will Clarkson
Peter C. Cornell Trust
Mary M. Dillon Estate
JoAnn Falletta and Robert Alemany
Mrs. Marion Fay
Robert J. and Martha B. Fierle Foundation
Charles J. Hahn
Daniel and Barbara Hart
Ms. Michele O. Heffernan & Mr. John J. Cordes
David and Lucinda Hohn
John and Janice Horn
Nancy Julian and Kenneth Schmieder
Warren W. and Virginia Lane
Mr. and Mrs. Leonard T. LoVullo
Sam and Anne Savarino
Roy and Ruth Seibel Family Foundation
Stephen and Monica Spaulding
Dr. and Mrs. Charles S. Tirone
Lorinda McAndrew Voelkle Foundation
Connie and Jack Walsh
Paul Zuydhoek and Tamar Halpern

*Deceased

PHOTO BY ENID BLOCH

BPO 75
BUFFALO PHILHARMONIC ORCHESTRA
A celebration of music in Buffalo, 1935-2010

On October 2, 2010 Music Director JoAnn Falletta took the podium in Kleinhans Music Hall to open the Orchestra's 75th Anniversary Celebration in the same manner as Lajos Shuk opened the first Buffalo Philharmonic Orchestra season on November 7, 1935 – by marking the downbeat of Beethoven's *Egmont* Overture.

Midori first performed as a guest soloist with the BPO on October 18, 1986. She appeared four more times between 1989 and 2001. How fitting that nearly a quarter of a century later she was on hand to perform Tchaikovsky's beloved Violin Concerto, helping launch the BPO's 75th Anniversary season with a flourish.

ILLUSTRATION INDEX

A special thanks to the Buffalo & Erie County Public Library, Grosvenor Room for the use of the wonderful Buffalo Philharmonic Scrapbook Collection, and to the Buffalo Philharmonic Orchestra for the BPO Archives.